God's
Fingernail

Rediscovering the Grace of Life's Lessons
by Jeffrey Skaret

God's Fingernail

Rediscovering the Grace of Life's Lessons

by

Jeffrey Skaret

Acknowledgements

—ᴍ—

I would like to acknowledge my parents, Patty and Norm, for instilling in me a foundation from which I have been able to live my life and write this book, and to my sister and brothers for helping to keep me grounded and connected throughout. I wish to thank Dr. Jackson Huntley, my college professor, mentor, and friend, who has guided and encouraged me through these many years. For their advice and encouragement early in this project, I would also like to thank Louise Woehrle and Ann Hunter, and for her gentle yet relentless nudging to get this published, Sarah Person. To my dear, life-long friends Michael Boylan, Mike Buysse, Mike Gallagher, Ricko Howells, Mark Muth, Tim Myers, Jon Schwingler, and Kevin Sorbo, your friendship and help have meant more to me than you'll ever fully know.

Finally, to Heidi, Christian and Cali, thank you for your patience, support, advice, enthusiasm, laughter, and love. You have often believed in me more than I have myself.

Contents

—m—

Introduction

—ᴍᴍ—

*A*s a middle-aged man caught up in the consuming realities of day-to-day life as a father, husband, and businessman, being jolted into another reality turned my world upside down. I was forced to abandon my routine and ambitions to face the unexpected, but sometimes that is when the greatest lessons of life are realized.

I was given the gift of perspective, recalling my life with my mother and father, growing up with my family, and remembering certain instances in which I was taught invaluable lessons of life. These lessons shaped me and helped to define me, mostly by how they were taught, what was said and what was done, and the examples that were set. I hadn't realized before just how much I had learned, or was to have learned, but these years later, at this defining moment, I was drawn to revisit my childhood experiences with a different set of eyes. I was led to reconsider what these lessons held for me and how they shaped who I've become.

God's Fingernail is the result. I now have a clearer picture. I used to go about my life from one day to the next, one project after another, moment upon moment, never really giving much thought to who I was or what I was doing, and why. Sure, I had goals, dreams, and aspirations. I had even been to seminars on positive thinking, personal development, and goal setting. But somehow the goals I would write down never really had that much pull. Assigning them value and compelling reasons always proved elusive, which made them harder to attain.

In rediscovering these lessons, I came to realize I had it mostly wrong. The goals I had for myself were mainly tangible and rather selfish, and that's why they didn't have much pull. I wasn't able to understand how and why others needed to somehow benefit from what I set out for myself. Through the event of my mother's unexpected massive heart attack, I received the blessing of a better understanding, not only of myself, but also of a much larger piece of living—and of dying.

The reflections on these memories, experiences, and lessons form the cornerstones of my foundation. But they are just that, *my* reflections forming *my* foundation. Your personal reflections and your realized foundation will be different, based on your own set of experiences and what you learned from them. My hope is that you may see a bit of yourself in these pages, but more that you will take the time to experience *your own* reflections of *your own* life and thus gain more insight into who you've become and why, and that those reflections may help guide you through the rest of your life as you seek to make a difference, both for yourself and for those around you.

*   *   *

Jeffrey Skaret was born and raised in Mound, Minnesota, surrounded by beautiful Lake Minnetonka. After living in a few places around the country, he and his wife settled back in Minnesota to raise their two children. God's Fingernail is Jeffrey's first book.

"Life is what happens to you while you are busy making other plans."
~John Lennon

Chapter One

Chapter One

—⁓—

**Life is what happens to you while you
are busy making other plans.**

— John Lennon

*B*loomington, Minnesota, 1997: Life was chaotic.
After a number of years and a few moves across
the country, we had made the decision to move back to
Minnesota to be closer to our families as we raised our
own children; but a full night's sleep had been elusive for
weeks, and this night wouldn't be much different. Driving
home, exhausted from another eighteen-hour day, as sleet
was turning the road to ice, I thought to myself, "*The
morning rush hour will be a mess*." It was late, nearly one
o'clock in the morning, but cars and trucks still crawled

along the freeway in a steady stream in both directions, unusual for the Twin Cities. This time of night midweek was typically quieter, more settled.

While putting in full days at my real job, I had been working late nights and weekends for several weeks, trying to speed up the reconstruction of the house we had bought. We started an addition and remodel in September and moved out in November, and now March loomed, reluctantly ushering in its fickle transition from long, cold Minnesota winter to sloppy, unpredictable Minnesota spring. Living in temporary quarters at Heidi's parents, we appreciated their hospitality and were thankful for their patience and understanding; but we were also growing weary living out of boxes and suitcases. After more than ten years of marriage and two young children, neither of us was eager to be sharing a house with parents. We needed our space. However, there we were, redesigning our lives and moving back to our geographic center, though it was not yet truly home.

Home is a relative term. For most, it is a place to feel welcomed, warm, and safe, a place to settle in and be content. Home is where we breathe in the comforting air of familiarity. As we move through life, we replace the scents, sounds, and memories from our childhood homes with new ones, those of our own. We create them unknowingly, but they become part of us and are comforting just the same. When we go back to our childhood homes, our senses spring to life in recognition of what was. Old memories waft through the air and into our minds, filling again the spaces with our earlier days. Some are vividly clear and have never been far from conscious thought, but others have been stashed away, reserved for another time and place to be resurrected when needed, often unexpectedly.

The Family

While we were working to reestablish our lives in a new place, my parents, Norm and Patty, were busy getting ready for a move to another chapter of theirs. It was time for them to prepare for retirement from years of working and raising four children, helping each of us through college and cheering our accomplishments along the way. They were eagerly going about their plans so they could spend winters in Arizona. Excited about the future, they were looking forward to having time to do what they wanted, watch their grandchildren grow, and cheer them along the way, too. They were ready for their new adventure.

Mine was a family of six—two parents, four children. In the younger days, it seemed as though we had two families combined into one. My sister Kristin and I were born two years apart in the latter half of the 1950s, she being the oldest. Many years later (seven to be precise, but it might as well have been twenty-seven because it was a lifetime to me then) my brother John was born. Fifteen months after that, Paul showed up. We had the same parents, and they have assured us there were no "accidents."

Those age gaps were more like chasms when we were young. When Kristin and I were in college, John and Paul were still finding their way through elementary school. When they were younger, I was often their babysitter and would trip them as they'd run around the house in their footie pajamas. They'd come running, one after the other, never knowing which wall I'd be lurking behind; then suddenly I'd stick my leg out and trip the first one, who would immediately plant face first into the carpet with the other toppling over him. We would all laugh and do it again until they bonked their heads together. I would make popcorn or dole out M&Ms—one for me, one for you; two for me, one for you; three for me, one for you—and the world would be better as we'd sit together on the couch and watch TV eating our treats. I'd hug them as I put them to bed, loving the way they wrapped their arms around my neck to say goodnight, and then I'd tap their sternum a few times with my knuckle, threatening to give them the old 99'er if they didn't pipe down. Then I'd tuck them in.

Kristin and I had always been close. I acted as her toy for awhile, I think. When we were very young, she would corral me and teach me new games, like how to dress Ken appropriately for a date with Barbie and how to do it *quickly* because "Barbie" didn't have a lot of patience. Or she would teach me how to organize and present a fun neighborhood carnival, where I could be the barker and announce the beautiful yet mysterious acrobat named Kristina the Magnificent and prepare the unsuspecting audience of four-, five-, and six-year-olds for her death-defying leg-hang from the top of the swing set.

As we got older I continued to fulfill a role for her as cameraman, stunt double, and general monkey boy as she wrote, directed, and starred in such classic indie films as *Cry-Out* (see *Laugh-In*), *The Winter of '72* (see *Summer of '42*), and *The Monster of Jessie Lake* (see *Godzilla*). I think my name as a contributor ended up in the very small, italicized print at the end of the credits, somewhere after something like "Copyright Kristin Productions MCMLXVIII."

Eventually, thankfully in many ways, the years passed and the gaps closed as we all found our way to adulthood, pursuing life on our own.

The Telephone

Entering through the front door of my in-laws, I stepped carefully so I wouldn't create a trail from the head-to-toe sheetrock dust covering me. Each night I tip-toed exactly the same path after taking off my boots: up the stairs, taking a right turn into the bathroom, and dropping my work clothes into a pile before climbing into the shower. After a quick rinse it was straight to the bedroom, where I would deftly slip under the covers, careful not to wake Heidi and eager to fall asleep for a few hours before the alarm went off again.

Off in the distance I could hear a telephone ringing. The sound became louder and closer until I awoke with a start and grabbed for the receiver. The room was pitch-dark, except for a green glow from the digital alarm clock. The numbers read 4:08. As I tried to shake the sleep from my brain, I picked up the phone with a thick, throaty, stammered, and confused "Hello?" knowing instinctively the call could not bring good news at four o'clock in the morning. Dad was on the other end of the line. His usually strong voice was quivering, saying "Jeff? It's Dad. Mom had a heart attack and—and—it doesn't look good. We had no warning—they—they—don't think she's going to make it." He cried. A swift and massive heart attack struck Mom while she was getting ready for bed upon arriving in Arizona, after their three-day drive from Minnesota.

I couldn't believe what I was hearing. It was surreal. It felt like a dream, strange and odd; the message is weird and doesn't register or make sense, but the experience is so intense it seems real. In dreams the innermost part of the mind can somehow pull you out of fantasy and back into reality. With dreams you may wake up with a pounding heart, but after a couple of deep breaths you can snuggle back under the covers, relieved it wasn't real.

But this wasn't a dream.

The gravity in Dad's voice made a chill rush down my spine, and it snapped me alert. I felt numb and didn't know what to say. He made it clear she wasn't likely to live. Through his soft sobs, through his fear and disbelief, he asked me to call my brothers and my sister to let them know and make arrangements for us to be with him in Arizona at her bedside as soon as possible.

The morning moved in slow motion. Nothing happened quickly enough, as precious minutes ticked away. Minutes turned into hours, painful, grinding hours. I had said a small prayer after hanging up the phone with Dad, but for the rest of the morning I was consumed with getting to Phoenix. Until the plane lifted off, there had been no time to think or reflect. The four of us were all strangely quiet, lost in our own thoughts as the reality of our journey was sinking in. I closed my eyes, stinging from emotion, and began to ask God silently for answers. Resting my head in the corner of the jet window and the seat back, I remembered.

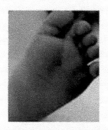

"I remember my mother's prayers and they have clung to me all my life."
~Abraham Lincoln

Chapter Two

Chapter Two

—ᨆ—

**I remember my mother's prayers and
they have clung to me all my life.**

—Abraham Lincoln

*M*y bed was pushed tightly against the walls in
the corner of my room when I was a young
boy. In summer I'd move my pillow to the other end so I
could lie beneath the opened window to look at the stars
and listen to the crickets. The moon was often crystal
clear and bright, shining its beam on the three apple trees
taking up a good chunk of our backyard. Everything was
more vivid at night back then. The stars were alive with
fire and brilliance, filling the skies much more than they
seem to now. The crickets were louder, yet the nights were

somehow quieter. There were no sirens piercing the night air and no phones ringing at odd hours. I was in my own home and in my own bed. I felt safe, and I felt loved.

It was during those times lying in bed, getting lost in the vastness of the warm summer night skies, that I would let my mind wander. I would think about the day I had and sometimes smile and laugh a little to myself. Sometimes I'd cry, but not often. I would say a little prayer, and at that age my prayers were short and to the point. I would thank God for *this*, ask Him to forgive me for *that*, but those were top-of-mind comments and always after the bedtime prayer I'd been taught:

"Now I lay me down to sleep, I pray the Lord my soul to keep. If I die before I wake. . ."

I always got a little hung up there. What did that mean, "If I die"? How would that happen? I was just a little kid. I didn't want to die in my sleep. In fact, I didn't want to die at all. Most nights I would breeze right through that part. I didn't want to give God or any*one* or any*thing* any ideas. They didn't need any help in figuring out ways to do me in.

I remembered being distracted from my prayers sometimes by the light of the moon. Of course, I could also be distracted from prayers by falling asleep or by thinking about the snakes under my bed or the monster in my closet. I hated them. They scared me. Most nights I would stand at the doorway of my room after I had brushed my teeth and rock back and forth, one foot in front of the other. After some experience of landing a little short, I knew how far I had to leap to get onto the bed in order to escape the serpents' reach, but I also had to consider how much time I had between flipping the light switch and making that leap. The snakes would never try to grab me with the light on, but as soon as it went out they could come out from under the bed and go for my ankles. Oh how I dreaded that! I was a pretty good leaper but not great. While I could never quite make it to the bed before it got dark in the room, I was still fast enough to get there before the snakes got me.

Safe under my covers and after calming my heart rate, I'd stare at the full moon and study, trying to imagine someone living there. The craters and lunar mountains formed interesting patterns, looking like earthly continents and vast oceans. When the moon was just a sliver, a crescent moon, I imagined it being God's fingernail. I figured He was keeping a hand on things, His finger on the pulse of the world, on the rhythm of life, just a subtle, gentle reminder that He is there. And I quaked a bit at the thought of Him always looking down at me, watching me, pointing at me with that fingernail.

I grew up in a churchgoing family. I was baptized in the hospital just hours after my birth, before the doctors performed hernia surgery on my little body. Mom and Dad wanted to be sure I had been sealed by the mark of the cross in case the surgery went awry. It didn't.

Every Sunday we went to church and listened to Lutheran sermons. I sat through Sunday school and sang in the youth choirs. Our choir director for the Carol Choir was Mrs. Lindle, and we were a rambunctious group of seven-to-ten-year-olds who gathered with her on Saturday mornings at St. John's Lutheran Church to practice. We were cute, with our little white robes that looked like table-cloths for card tables with holes cut through the middle of them for our heads to fit through. And we wore huge red bows that nearly covered our faces, wrapping up around our heads and framing our cheeks so we looked a lot like those poppies veterans hand out on Veterans Day for a modest donation. We were pretty good singers, as most of us could carry a tune, but Mrs. Lindle was elderly and a bit hard of hearing, which was interesting for a choir director now that I think about it. And she had a very thick, unidentifiable accent from some other part of the world, and we would find all kinds of reasons to give her a hard time about it. When she'd say things like "Children! Please!" it sounded like "chaul dra paleece!" and we'd ask her why she was calling the police. I don't know how she did it all those years, but she was clearly a good heart and a dedicated, beautiful person who only wanted to have her choir of young children's voices fill the sanctuary on Sundays with songs like "This is My Father's World" and "This Little Light of Mine."

Through it all, the Saturday practices and donning the silly robes for Sunday services were really just dress rehearsals for the grandest of all performances: the Christmas Eve Musical Splendor.

Ah, the *Splendor*! No other performance throughout the year compared to it. We worked on songs for it year-round, with Mrs. Lindle making the final decision on which two songs we were to sing for that night; but one of them was always "Venite Adoremus," which was Mrs. Lindle's signature piece for us. Actually, we sang two songs on our own and a third was part of the grand finale, in which we joined vocal forces with the Senior Choir, the Choralettes, and the Youth Choir. The Senior Choir was the main church choir, made up of adults of all ages who could carry a tune. The Choralettes were a group of a dozen or so women who were a lot jazzier than the Senior Choir and, unfortunately, not nearly as polished. I think their standards for membership were pretty loose, welcoming anybody who wanted to raise their voice in praise regardless of their ability to sing on key. The Youth Choir consisted of junior and senior high students, most of whom also sang in their school choirs. They could sing on key.

I always looked forward to the Splendor, even the prospect of getting up in front of a packed Christmas Eve sanctuary singing my little heart out. Every set of eyes were fixed on us, and it was intimidating as I hoped upon hope that I wouldn't forget the words or pass out like Jimmy Dempster did a couple of years earlier. I guess the Norwegian lutefisk his grandparents made him try that Christmas Eve didn't set well. For those who don't know or have never tried it, lutefisk is white fish, like cod, skinned, deboned, salted, and then hung out to dry for several weeks until it hardens and smells like the inside of your eighty-eight-year-old great uncle's shoe. It is then dumped into a bucket and soaked in lye (yes, the very same lye used to make soap). After floating around in that for several days, a gelatinous goo coats it so that when the fish is eaten no chewing is necessary and it can glide right down the esophagus toward an unsuspecting stomach. Jimmy's stomach acted as it should have, and I vowed to stay away from lutefisk.

Jimmy's experience notwithstanding, there was something special about that night. Everyone was smiling. With evergreen boughs lining the perimeter of the ceiling and an eighteen-foot Christmas tree framing the right side of the altar, the church was filled with the scent of pine. The sanctuary was dimly lit, illuminated only by the candles placed at each row of pews and on the altar. There was a certain aura of calm and reverence that filled the air.

Near the end, as the organ began to gently roll over the notes of "Silent Night," every parishioner and every choir member, every usher, acolyte, and pastor, held a single candle in silence. One by one the candles would be lit by one person tipping his wick to touch the next person's flame. Standing on those altar steps and watching the light make its way across the congregation made something stir within me. I saw people standing elbow to elbow, some with children in their arms, and a few I knew to be alone, but all sharing the light. And as we all joined together to sing "Silent Night," smiles crept across the faces, and the voices of the people swelled into the most beautiful of choirs singing praise to the greatest light of all. A merry Christmas indeed.

Kris and I, as well as John and Paul, all sang in the Carol Choir when we were at those ages, and we all went through confirmation at that church, which was the very same church my parents had grown up in. It was part of our life and part of our routine, as much as our going to school. We were taught the prayers and would recite them dutifully in church, before meals, and at bedtime.

At some point during my youth, Mom began hosting Bible studies in our home on Monday nights. The group consisted mainly of women, women of all ages, from late teens and early twenty-somethings to women my mom's age and older. Occasionally there would be a young man or two in attendance, but I think they were there mainly for the young women.

There was a change in Mom. She and a couple of her close friends had begun to explore the Bible more deeply, more regularly, strengthening their faith and increasing their involvement in and around the church. She was more committed to her faith than what I had seen before, and at one point, at age seven or eight, I made the mistake of telling her and one of her friends as they chatted over coffee that I didn't want to go to Bible school in the summer for a whole week.

"Really. Why?" they asked.

"I don't know. I don't have time, I guess," I said. After all, I was playing baseball, riding bikes, catching frogs, and hanging with my friends. I couldn't take a whole week of mornings and hang out at church. I was busy.

Uh oh. I said the wrong thing, and I knew it as soon as the words left my lips. I wanted to grab them and pull them back before they reached their ears.

"Rats! How could I be so stupid?" I thought.

"You don't have time for God?" Mom asked. "Hmmm. That's a shame. I know God always has time for you."

"Oh boy," I thought to myself, *"now what?"*

Mom and her friend were looking at me, their tender eyes (really, they *were* tender) piercing my very soul and making me a bit squeamish. I wanted to run.

"Um, well, I really mean that I think I'm too old for Bible school. Most of the kids are like three and four or maybe six years old. None of my friends go anymore. Sure

I have time for God, I mean, but I've kinda done all the Bible school stuff. Don'tcha think?"

"Oh," Mom said.

My hand was already on the handle of the door to go outside as I said, "Uh, I'll see ya later. OK?" And with that I was out the door as fast as I could go, hoping against hope I could dodge Bible school for good.

When I got a little older, Mom began inviting me to the Bible studies on Monday nights. Again, *"Oh boy."* First, I had homework. Plus, there was this new thing called **Monday Night Football** coming on right after **Laugh-In**. And what about playing night games with my friends? Fall was the best time for that, and in the winter there was hockey and sledding. I had a lot of stuff to do.

Eventually my homework excuse wore thin, and the others were not really valid reasons for not being in the living room, sitting in a circle, reading and discussing passages from the Bible. My sister, Kris, was joining the group and had already told me they all heard me singing along with Sammy Davis Jr. on **Laugh-In** the week earlier. I was supposed to have been sick, but there I was, downstairs belting out "Spinning Wheel" right along with Sammy as he sang "What go-oes up, must co-ome down," apparently loud enough for the Bible group to hear.

Embarrassing, yes, and I felt guilty enough for ducking the study for so long that the next week I plopped myself in the living room with my Bible, ready for in-depth learning and introspection, hoping no one would ask me to sing Sammy's hit, "The Candy Man."

I was twelve or thirteen years old sitting through three consecutive Mondays of Bible study. I didn't like it. I didn't get it. It was over my head, all of it. They would try to include me in the discussion, asking me questions, wondering what I thought. What did I know? I was just a kid trying to make it through the session so I could get a cookie or a cupcake and catch the end of the football game on TV with Dad.

I don't remember exactly how I got out of it altogether, but I think I just leveled with Mom, telling her I didn't "get" most of the discussions. We talked about it for a while, and she let me off the hook, saying she understood.

Still, I sort of felt like I was missing something, like I was *supposed* to be able to understand and participate, like I was *supposed* to care about all of that more than I did. I'm not sure I felt guilty as much as I felt confused and intimidated. It took me a good week or two before being totally comfortable sitting downstairs and watching **Laugh-In** and **Monday Night Football** again. No more singing, though, and I was sure not to go back upstairs until everyone had left.

For some reason my knowledge of and relationship with God now became more complicated, more confusing, and less certain than when I was younger. I had been content in my simple understanding that there was a God and that I needed to praise Him, love Him, and fear Him. Mostly in my simple understanding, I knew He loved *me*. That had been good enough for me and allowed me to be myself when I said my personal bedtime prayers, which were tacked onto the end of "Now I lay me down to sleep" with an "Oh yeah, and God?" as if trying to catch Him before tuning out to listen to someone else's prayer.

Mom always told me God could see everything and hear everyone all the time. He never tuned out. Not only was that hard to imagine, but it was also a bit ominous. I mean, my parents had eyes in the backs of their heads for sure, but how was it possible for God to actually hear *everything* and *everyone* all the time? Anyway, He might think it ill-mannered of me to just assume He was still listening. Who was I to think I was so important that He'd just sit around and wait for me to talk to Him?

Later in life I came to understand that to be one of the things God does really well. Mom helped me learn that during a time when I didn't think He was listening to me at all.

*   *   *

Reflection

Take one step at a time. Life is full of conflict, contradictions, confusion, and choices; some are self-inflicted, and some are thrust upon me. At times I feel pressure to know more and to be more than I can or want at a given moment—to leap three or four steps at once. Sometimes I'm just not ready. It's easy to see that in myself; the hard part is recognizing it in others and allowing them to take their own steps in their own time.

*   *   *

Phoenix

As the plane touched down, my heart began to beat more rapidly in fear and trepidation. Kent and Bob, friends of our parents, met us at the airport with expressionless faces and somber greetings. Their demeanor gave us no indication, so we had to ask whether Mom was still alive. She was, but there was no more good news than that.

Anticipation and anxiety were thick in the car as the big, tan sedan lumbered onto the freeway for the forty-minute ride to the hospital. There were many questions, but few were asked. There were fewer answers. It was quiet. Air in the car was stifling, heavy and looming, almost suffocating from silence and tension mixing with the hot, midday Arizona sun. Halfhearted attempts at chat broke the silence but fell uselessly around me and only made the seemingly endless trip longer. None of it mattered. My mind never strayed far from the thoughts that had been consuming me since the early morning hours. As I watched the lines on the freeway disappear beneath the car, my mind drifted and I remembered.

"A hero is someone who understands the responsibility that comes with his freedom."
~Bob Dylan

Chapter Three

Chapter Three

—⚉—

A hero is someone who understands the responsibility that comes with his freedom.

— Bob Dylan

*M*om would often tell me how much I reminded her of her father, Grandpa Pat. She spoke so fondly of him and would tell me how proud he would be of me if he were alive. He used to gather me in his arms and plop me on his lap saying, "When you get big and I get small, then we'll have a time!" I smiled softly as I thought of him and the small stone he kept in his pocket. It was worn smooth from years of rubbing and touching and rolling between his fingers. It was always with him.

He came to America on a boat from Sweden as a young man in 1910. I've seen pictures and film clips of immigrants over the years and have noticed how many of them raise their arms in joy and relief upon arrival. Some drop to their knees and look toward heaven to offer thanks. Others kiss the ground the moment they feel American soil beneath their feet. Grandpa picked up a stone. He never wanted to forget the feeling he had when he stepped off that ship. He never wanted to forget the promises he made to himself.

He put the stone in his pocket, and there it stayed. I didn't think much about it until later in my life, years after he had passed away. Mom had kept the stone, along with his small coin collection and some old photographs, in a worn-out shoe box with two rubber bands holding its tattered cover in place. Every so often she would slide the box out from underneath the bed and show me something different she had come across or relay another story she remembered. Sometimes she would tell me a story she had told before. I must admit that bothered me as I got older, but when I was young I wanted to hear the stories again and again. Always, she would put the stone in my hand as we went through the memories. Eventually, she

46

gave it to me after having it mounted on royal blue velvet and set in a small wooden frame, protected beneath glass. A brass nameplate identifies it, stating simply "Grandpa Pat's Rock 1901." It was supposed to read "1910," but the engraver made a mistake, and Mom didn't notice it until after it was mounted, sealed in its case, and given to me as a gift. I now have it in my office, and in my mind I draw an imaginary line with an arrow, moving the "1" in front of the "0," knowing it is really supposed to be "1910."

He died when I was nine. It was the first funeral I had ever been to, and I didn't fully understand what was happening. I remember being very sad and very scared. I remember looking at him in the casket, quite certain I saw his finger move, and thinking that any minute he'd get up and make a joke and a vat of vegetable soup. He was a cook. No, a chef, an artist of the everyman meal, and he took great pride in doing what he loved. He had run his own café, the Del-O, and then became in charge of the entire cafeteria at the Tonka Toys factory, where his homemade soups and Swedish meatballs were always in high demand. He would have me come around into the kitchen and watch him chop vegetables or hand me one of his long-handled spoons and let me stir the soup. He was a fortunate man, and I was a fortunate grandson.

When he died, I was wrapped up in a young boy's kind of life. My world was pretty much just that—my world. The night of his passing was an understandably difficult one for Mom and Dad, and looking back I realize I probably made it more so by my lack of reaction when given the news. What activity I had planned I don't care to recall, but Mom's sadness was clear in my mind as I remember leaving the house that night. What she wanted and needed most at that moment was the support and love of her family. She needed me to be there, to hold onto her. I knew this because that was what I was feeling every inch of my journey to her now.

*   *   *

Reflection

Be an example. My grandfather had clear goals and expectations. That doesn't mean they were easy. It means they were very clear in his mind. He seemed to know who he was, what he wanted out of life, and what he expected of himself. Those are core challenges and questions, but he had a tangible reminder, that stone in his pocket, which served to help keep him well grounded and well focused. And that stone now reminds me of my own goals and expectations. It reminds me that I have a role in something much larger than myself and I need to do my part and be an example, just as my Grandpa Pat remains for me.

*   *   *

The Hospital

As we turned off the freeway and onto the boulevard, signs for the hospital began to appear. We went past the main entrance and turned into the area marked "EMERGENCY AND INTENSIVE CARE." Dad was waiting near the doors and stepped forward as he saw the sedan approach. I could see the burden pressing down on his shoulders, as he slowly moved from the shadows of the building to wait for the car to stop. Standing in the bright afternoon sun, his face told of the night he had been through. His eyes were swollen and red from a lack of sleep and the flow of tears. His thinning gray hair was disheveled and his beard unshaven, white whiskers peeking from his tanned face.

The car stopped, and all four doors opened as we hurried to get out and into his arms. There the four of us surrounded him, hugged him, and sobbed. Dad wept and gathered us closer. In embracing him, the severity of Mom's condition was immediately felt. It was as though he was reaching out, grasping, collecting energy and strength from each of us to deliver to her because he no longer had enough by himself. He was weary, drained from this emotional nightmare but relieved and thankful we had come.

We walked through the double glass doors and into the corridor. Dad led us past the sign reading "INTENSIVE CARE" into a small waiting room where a middle-aged couple huddled next to an elderly woman, whispering and gently patting her on the back. The man turned his head slowly and nodded a solemn greeting in our direction, as in empathy and understanding of what was to come. We passed through a set of heavy doors, and they closed quietly behind us, latching with a muffled clap. Absence of normal conversation made the intensive care unit noticeably quiet. Still, it was deafening from the constant humming, buzzing, and beeping of monitors and other machines.

Nothing could have prepared us for the impact of seeing Mom lying unconscious, breathing only with the aid of a machine rhythmically pumping oxygen into her lungs. Her chest heaved and fell with every hiss and click of the device. She didn't look like herself. Her speckled gray hair was matted against her head and there were tubes in her arms, in her mouth, and in her nose. Wires were running in every direction. We moved slowly to gather around the bed, carefully avoiding the machines keeping her alive.

The room was stark with one blue, vinyl-covered chair at the foot of the bed and another near Mom's side. In a corner out of easy reach stood a small cabinet of drawers with tissue, a simple vase holding a very small bouquet of cut flowers, and a Bible set atop. I wondered to myself why the room was so large, with part of it curtained off and a lonely machine of some sort standing idly in its center. What else did they do in there?

A nurse quietly greeted us, pulled a heavy curtain across the floor to ceiling windows facing the nurse's station for privacy, and introduced herself as Marianne. She left the five of us silently standing around Mom's bed with tears streaming down our faces.

Each of us touched her. I stroked her forehead and leaned down to softly kiss her cheek. Her olive skin had faded to ashen but was warm to my lips. As a tear fell from my eyes onto her cheek, I slowly wiped it away with my forefinger and could think of nothing other than how much I loved her. I held her hand and my mind flashed.

"I don't like that man. I must get to know him better."
~Abraham Lincoln

Chapter Four

Chapter Four

—∞—

I don't like that man. I must get to know him better.

—Abraham Lincoln

I grew up in a neighborhood filled with kids. There was always activity, with a bunch of us usually gathering across three connected backyards. There were no fences, trees, or hedges separating them, providing an adequate field for football, baseball, tag, or any other loosely organized fun.

There are always one or two kids in a neighborhood who take charge. Usually they are the oldest, maybe the biggest, but they undoubtedly wield the most authority. In our neighborhood there was Big Tanner. Intimidating and controlling, he was the organizer. He had final say on everything, right or wrong. But of course he was always right, and he made sure everyone understood that.

One sunny, early spring Saturday afternoon, a bunch of us were gathering across the backyards for a pickup game of baseball. Our ages ranged from seven or eight years old to about fourteen. The older guys, Big Tanner and Greg, were always the self-appointed captains. Big Tanner grabbed the Louisville Slugger bat with Mickey Mantle's signature burned into the barrel. His right hand gripped it in the middle, and Greg's hand went on the handle above his. Then Big Tanner's hand, then Greg's, and so on until Big Tanner held only the knob of the bat by his fingers. If Greg could kick the bat out of his hands with one kick, he could choose the first player. He couldn't. In fact, Big Tanner was the only one who could kick the bat out of someone's grip, so he always chose first whether he did the kicking or the holding. I wondered why we went through that ritual each and every time when the outcome was never really in doubt, although I suppose there was always the hope something could change. Alternately, they began choosing their teammates, the best players first.

As the last few kids were being unceremoniously selected, my cousin Sandy came running down the hill, ducking beneath the overgrown hedge and into the yards with her leather All-Star glove in hand. All-Star gloves could be bought at the local hardware store, and even though they didn't cost much, they were made of real leather and bore the autograph of a major league ballplayer. Mine held the signature of Ron Santo, Cubs third baseman, but most of the major leaguers they got to sign them were not real all-stars. They were the kind of players you only knew if one of them happened to be on your favorite team. I think Sandy's held the name of Ted Uhlaender, a reserve outfielder for the Twins. He became her favorite player. That was a good deal for Ted.

While Greg's team was heading for home plate to bat and Big Tanner was assigning positions to us, Sandy hollered out, "Hey! Whose team can I be on?" She was out of breath, but her eyes were bright with anticipation as she bounded onto the field. Someone yelled for her to go on Greg's team, but as that was being said, Big Tanner spoke above everyone.

"You can't play!" he shouted.

Quickly, Sandy asked "Why?"

Before anyone else could speak, Big Tanner moved toward her and stood within inches of her, looking down on her like a towering giant.

As Sandy looked up, he said firmly, "The teams are even."

"But—" Sandy tried to respond.

Big Tanner then said again, "YOU can't play!"

"Why?" Sandy asked, trying to understand.

Numbers of players never mattered before. It didn't matter if one team had an extra fielder. Most of the younger ones couldn't catch or throw very well anyway, and neither could Kenny Klingenfeather, who was twelve and viewed more as a novelty than an athlete. I think he was left-handed, but he threw the same awful way with both arms, so it was really hard to tell. One more or one less fielder didn't matter.

"BECAUSE YOU'RE AN OHLER!" Big Tanner boomed.

That was Sandy's last name. Our mothers were sisters. Her eyes filled with tears as she stood beneath Tanner's icy glare. Others were chiming in, jeering and laughing, and Sandy looked around, confused. She turned away and ran back up the hill toward her house crying, disappearing beyond the hedge.

I didn't do anything. I didn't say anything. I just stood there, stunned.

Everyone else seemed to act as if nothing unusual happened and eagerly went about starting the game. I felt weak and began wandering off the field. A couple of kids yelled, "Hey! Where ya goin'?" and Tanner yelled, "Get back out there!"

My good buddy Charlie, whose family owned one of the backyards, asked as I walked by, "Forget somethin'?" I said simply, meekly, "I gotta go," as I found my way to my bike.

My legs were heavy, as if trudging through mud or thigh-deep snow. I could hear my friends hollering in my direction, some imploring me to stay, and others mocking me, calling me a baby and a quitter. As I slipped my base-ball glove over the butterfly handlebars, I felt numb. A buzz started to crawl over my body. I climbed onto my fake leopard skin, banana-shaped seat and began to pedal. The baseball cards stuck onto my spokes with Mom's clothespins clicked along slowly and methodically at first but began to clatter more rapidly and loudly as I pedaled faster to keep up with my racing, pounding heart. My eyes were beginning to glaze over, and I was having trouble

59

breathing. I was panting, unable to catch my breath. Rounding the curve to head up the slight incline toward my house, I veered unexpectedly into our neighbor's yard and tipped over into their bushes.

Beneath the tangled branches that had poked and scratched me on my way down, I could hear the wheels of my bike clicking their way to a slow stop. I could not catch my breath or see clearly. I lay on my back beneath the shrubs for some time, eventually rolling to my side to put my hands on the ground and push myself up. Still feeling a bit wobbly, I grabbed the handlebars and began to push my bike up the grassy side of the hill toward our garage and parked it cradled between our rusty red wheelbarrow and my sister's moss-green bike with the wire saddle baskets and flared fenders. I entered the house through the basement garage door and flopped face down on the couch with my arms outstretched, feeling the cool musty air as it settled onto my hot, sweaty skin.

I don't remember much else about the evening until I went to bed, lying with my head beneath the window. Looking out at the night sky with faint moonglow peeking through wispy clouds, I remembered the day and began to whimper. I told myself to stop and asked why. Why hadn't

I said something? Why did they have to pick on her? Why were they so mean? Why didn't I do something? Why did I feel so alone?

Looking back, I must have been tossing and turning for a while, and I must have been more than whimpering because the door of my bedroom opened quietly, casting light from the hallway into my eyes. As I squinted at the silhouette in the doorframe, Mom came in and sat beside me on my bed. Without a word she kissed my forehead and stroked my cheek with the back of her hand. She then wrapped her arms around me and held me. We sat like that for a few minutes until finally she whispered, "What's wrong, honey?" At first I told her nothing was wrong. She was silent and just held me. Then as I told her of the day, I began to cry all over again. She rocked me.

I blamed myself for not stepping in and saying something, for not defending Sandy. I felt horrible for letting her down. Mom listened. Choosing her words carefully, she told me, "The most important thing when someone is hurting is to be there for them. Be with them. Sometimes you don't need to say anything. Just be with them."

* * *

Reflection

Be a friend. Empathy and understanding are attributes to be nurtured in the young and treasured in adults. I had it as a kid, then lost a bit of it in my early adult years as I focused on myself and my own desires to achieve and become. Meeting others where they are is a key to gaining insight and understanding of another perspective, for I have found myself in similar places throughout my life, needing a sympathetic ear and an empathetic hug.

*   *   *

Reality Check

I moved to the chair at the side of Mom's bed and sat down, wrapping my hands around hers. My brother John began to say a prayer aloud. Choking back tears his voice trailed off, and Paul picked it up. It was a strange set of moments. There was frustration, anger, helplessness, and sadness in the room as Kris blurted out "Why? Why now? This isn't fair!"

All of it was raw. I hadn't been through anything like this before, so it was a new roller coaster of emotions. It was difficult to take, but what made this even more intense was seeing the others' emotions so unmasked. It was hard enough to manage and make sense of my own, but I was forced to witness and live through the emotions of others, and they weren't just like mine. We were all trying to come to grips with this circumstance thrust upon us, new to each of us. I was mostly sad, not angry. But there was a sense of anger in the room, and it was weird, each of us equally traumatized and handling things in our own way. We had been jerked away from the lives we were building. Our sense of family and comfort, our plans, had been derailed by this unfair and unexpected event. Each of us had been going about raising our families, working and looking toward the future, wanting to replicate in some manner the lives we had known and wanted for our own families. This was not as it should be with Dad weeping, his hands clasped tightly together, pressed against his forehead.

Nurse Marianne came in to check on the machines and tubes. As she did, she said, "Thank you. Thank you for coming so quickly." She continued to push buttons and make adjustments saying, "Your parents need you. Both of them."

After a few moments, we asked Marianne if she could tell us exactly what happened and what we could expect. She said, "Your mother suffered a massive and damaging heart attack. She slipped into a coma on her way to the hospital last night. She is in a very precarious state." She sounded patronizing, as if we didn't already know that. "The doctor is aware you are here and will be in shortly to speak with you."

"*Ohhhh-kaaay*," I thought to myself.

Some minutes later there was a gentle rapping on the door, and Dr. Naswarii stepped in to introduce himself. He was a pleasant-looking man with a brown complexion, black hair and dark, soft, kind eyes framed by bushy black eyebrows. The stiff white coat was in stark contrast to his appearance and demeanor. He was thoughtful and deliberate as he described the events leading to Mom's condition. The initial heart attack had damaged nearly seventy percent of the heart muscle. The emergency medical technicians dispatched to her needed to shock her heart with paddles numerous times to get it started again. She had been without oxygen flowing regularly to her brain for nearly fifteen minutes. Once in the hospital she suffered another heart attack. They needed to put the paddles to her twice more to revive her. Her heart and body had taken quite a beating, and additional fears were setting in because of fluid collecting in her chest.

"There are three areas of concern with your mother," he stated with a distinct Indian accent. "One is the condition of her heart and how much of it can function. Another is the fluid building in her chest, and third is the lack of oxygen to her brain." He was waiting for updated reports and x-rays, which would better determine what all of that meant, and would return after that time.

The doctor seemed gentle and genuine, not one of those cold, matter-of-fact types who appear detached and uninterested in the human experience. While there was not much in the way of encouraging news in his first visit with us, he did leave an impression of competence. Marianne assured us he would return soon as she walked out the door, closing it behind her. Looking at Dad, I began to think about my parents' life together.

"Take care of all your memories, for you cannot relive them."
~Bob Dylan

Chapter Five

Chapter Five

—⚊—

Take care of all your memories, for you cannot relive them.

—Bob Dylan

*T*hey were high school sweethearts. Patty wrote in a public guest book somewhere that she would someday marry Norm, signing her name as if she already had. Forty years of marriage had gone by quickly, raising four children who now had children of their own, and retirement was something they had been looking forward to. The trip to Arizona was using a month's vacation time Mom had accrued at her job, and they were making plans to spend the entire winter down there the following year. They had just sold the family home, bought a maintenance-free condominium, moved, and were going to buy a small winter home outside of Phoenix.

They spent weeks sifting through forty-some years of accumulated stuff, dividing much of it among us kids and some nephews and nieces. Some things were donated to church, and lots of other things were discarded. The sorting, throwing away, and disseminating of life's accumulations was as difficult for Mom and Dad as the selling of the house.

Letting go is hard.

Mom had taken turns with each of us, going through keepsakes she treasured, commemorating certain times in our lives. I don't know how deliberate she was with the others (I would guess quite), but with me it was a methodical reconstruction of much of my childhood. We started with my baby book, which faithfully noted the first two years of my life, including the precarious hernia surgery just days after my birth. I was told that kind of thing is tough on little babies.

Entries became less frequent after year four or five and were eventually skipped altogether until my confirmation when I was fourteen. We laughed out loud when I scolded her for not being more diligent in her chronicles.

"Hey. Wait a minute," I said. "There are all these blank pages. Look! Six, seven, eight, nine—what the heck? Nothing! You mean nothing interesting happened when I was six? Didn't I go to school for the first time that year? Didn't I say anything funny? Get a tooth knocked out or something? What could possibly have been so important during those years to distract you from your motherly duty of writing about me?"

Dad walked in and asked what was so funny. As we told him, he was drawn to recall a few things himself, like the time he and I hunted ducks down the Bigfork River, just the two of us on a cloudy, cool, quiet October day, drifting lazily down the river in a canoe. I was in front literally riding shotgun with Dad manning the paddle, managing the current, and navigating the bends of the river. I was eager with anticipation and excitement, fully expecting a flock of ducks to take wing at every turn. The Bigfork was pristine and lonesome yet full of rhythm and life at the same time. Fiery orange, sunburst yellow, and deep, crimson-red leaves clung desperately to the poplar, birch, and maple tree branches before letting go and floating helplessly into the river and onto the banks guiding its waters. Stands of full-bodied spruce and tall white pine framed the river and led to my wondering what natural mysteries they were protecting from my view. A doe stepped into the shallows of a backwater cove to get a drink with her fawn. A pair of mink scurried along the shoreline beneath an overhanging bank of wild grasses, wishing they hadn't been seen. And yes, we did get a few ducks that day.

It was one of those powerful bonding experiences between a father and a son that are all too rare for many. It was a shared experience, uninterrupted, and so memorable it's as if time was suspended, lasting far longer than the day itself.

I brought up how much I appreciated working for him at the cabinet shop. It was a business started by his Norwegian immigrant father in 1946. Grandpa Andy was a true craftsman, starting his business with nothing more than the skill and determination he brought with him from Norway. When the banker asked him what collateral he had for the loan to buy his building and saws, Grandpa looked down, then held his hands forward saying, "These." Grandpa had a shortened thumb and two fingers whacked off, one at the first knuckle and the other at the second, from three separate incidents at a table saw as he fed lumber through it working for a window and sash company a few years earlier. He figured if he was going to lose digits and risk limbs, he was going to do it for himself, not someone else. He got the loan.

Those fingers always served as a silent warning and a reminder for me from the time I was a little kid through when I worked there as a teen, first sweeping floors and cleaning out sawdust bins. Later I was promoted to "catcher-of-the-pieces-coming-off-the-saw-from-Vern" (a title too big to fit on a business card). Vern was a rapid-pace cabinet man with a serious demeanor and a part of the shop all to himself. They always put the young, green workers in for a stint with Vern before letting them loose in the rest of the shop. Vern was dedicated and reflected the work ethic of the place better than anyone, and that was all the training one needed to get off on the right foot. Respect the saw. Respect the day's work. Respect the business.

Dad told me he was glad I had a chance to work at the shop during those summers and to be there for my grand-father as well. Grandpa Andy was proud to have three generations working in a business he had started, in a craft and skill he had handed down. When I was in college, Dad and my uncle decided to close the business they had grown up in. The year was 1978, and along with double-digit inflation, sky-high interest rates, and lines at the gas pump, there was a dramatic slow-down in new apartment buildings, home construction, and remodeling. It was a very difficult decision for them to make. It can be hard to let go.

There was a pause of silence for a few moments as Mom sifted through a few more pieces of memorabilia. Dad sat down on the edge of the bed, and as I looked at him I saw the scars on his neck that I had seen nearly every day since I was eight years old. I thought how fortunate I was to have grown up with him in my life. He was a good father.

*　＊　＊　＊*

Reflection

Know where you came from. Much of whom I've become and why can be traced to experiences and memories seared into my subconscious, such as the work ethic and commitment set by my father and grandfather. My perspectives are uniquely mine, and my mind latches onto certain things and lets other things slip away. Yet I am shaped, molded, and even defined by those memories to which I cling.

"Nothing is more memorable then a smell."
~Diane Ackerman

Chapter Six

Chapter Six

—⟋⟍—

Nothing is more memorable than a smell.

— Diane Ackerman

When I was young, we used to spend a fall weekend or two cleaning up the yard, raking and mowing for the last time and putting away summer toys and tools. I really hated doing that for all kinds of reasons. For one, it meant the end of summer and the coming of winter, which always seemed to last a lot longer than summer. Second, I wasn't too keen on the work. Raking was monotonous, boring, and it seemed never-ending. And why should I have to do things like run around and pick up little plastic buckets and shovels from the sand box while dodging litter droppings from feral neighborhood cats? I was told it was all necessary and that it was good family bonding time.

"Family time, shmamily time. I'll get you some bonding time all right. I get plenty of that every day," I'd mumble to myself.

Looking back, however, I did appreciate a few things about those chores. The cool autumn air was filled with aromas and sounds reserved for that time of year. Sounds travel farther and are heard more clearly in the fall air, like those of a college football game blasted through the AM dial of the radio. The unmistakable play calling of Ray Christiansen, voice of the Golden Gophers, reverberated throughout the neighborhood, accompanied by the scratching of rakes, rumbling of lawn mowers, and an occasional barking of an order . . . or barking of a dog.

And there was laughter. Usually it was the gleeful play of children diving into leaf piles their parents had raked up. Every once in a while, a parent would take a break from raking and the serious task of winter preparation to also jump into a pile of leaves, just like the kids.

The leaves of fall have their own aroma. As they drift to the ground, dry up, and are strewn across the yard, there is a certain musky scent that comes from them. The aroma is stronger and more memorable when they are together, raked into a pile. Their sweet muskiness is always the same. Year after year it does not change, and each time I catch a whiff of it, I am brought immediately back to my childhood.

Some neighbors bagged leaves, while some raked them into compost areas. Most others in those days had designated a corner of their yard for burning them. That's what we did, and as we raked we would add the leaves and dead grass to the smoldering pile and watch as sparks would catch the new stuff, gradually turning embers into gentle, manageable flames methodically engulfing the newly added fuel and sending sweet-smelling wafts of smoke into the cool, crisp October air. That's what I liked: the fire, adding stuff to the pile, and watching the fire reenergize, while making certain the flames did not escape their boundaries. I would coax it along, just to the edge of where it should be and then quickly scold it for venturing too far, smacking it with my rake and stomping on it with my foot. There was a sense of control and satisfaction that came with that. Fire is sneaky and unpredictable, but standing there with a steel rake and managing its direction and consumption is somehow empowering and exciting and mesmerizing and calming at the same time. It sounds a little strange, but I never played with fire otherwise, except that one time with Mark Davis, burning ants with farmer matches he stole from his dad. But we got scared because some leaves caught on fire, taking off too quickly in the little woods down by his house. We panicked and started running and jumping around like maniacs, stomping on it, and kicking dirt to cover it up. Somebody saw us and told our parents. I don't know what happened to Mark, but my punishment was a severe tongue-lashing and a smack on the behind with a wooden spoon by Mom, followed by a brief lecture and a good swat on the behind by Dad when he got home from work. I was probably five years old and was told never to play with matches again. The next time we used magnifying glasses instead.

When I was eight we were spending a Saturday doing our yard work. We had a wire fence line surrounding the perimeter, with scallops on the top of it that were bent and misshapen from our climbing and crawling over it to retrieve various balls from various sports that were sent into the neighbors' yards over the years. While serving as a particularly good homerun fence for whiffle ball and a solid field boundary for football, it also served as a safe haven for grass and weeds that could not be reached by the mower. So by the time October rolled around, there was quite a tangled collection of leaves intertwined with long grass and uncontrolled weed infections winding all along the base of the fence surrounding our backyard.

Dad had a system, each year pouring a light stream of gasoline along the fence line to help speed the burn and destroy some of the twisted, choking leaves and weeds. It would work beautifully as he methodically kept the gas well ahead of the approaching flames. As the fire crept toward the new fuel it would catch quickly and evenly spread along the intended path, devouring what was in its way.

This particular year held nothing different, except that nearly one-year-old baby John waddled and crawled around in the grass playing with caterpillars and eating dirt, not helping much, and Mom was five or six months pregnant with Paul. In good shape and in good spirits, Mom handled the chores as usual and directed Kris and me to do our parts, all the while keeping an eye on baby John and making sure he remained occupied and out of trouble. I guess eating dirt was OK.

Suddenly, breaking the calm and familiarity of the day, came a muffled "AAHWHOOOF!" like an explosion of sorts. It made the ground shake. It was the kind of sound that is low and deep, exploding at its peak. And it reverberates in your chest. As he screamed out in his surprise, Dad stood there for a split moment and then began to run. I stood in disbelief of what I was seeing. It all happened so quickly. I saw Dad's head and chest engulfed in flames and heard Mom yelling his name as she ran toward him screaming, "Roll on the ground! Roll on the ground!" Within seconds she caught up to him as he was running toward the house, and she jumped on his back, six months pregnant and all, tackling him and knocking him to the ground. She was yelling, "Roll! Roll! Roll!" all the while pushing him and rolling him, tearing his shirt apart and calling for water. The stench of panic, burned flannel, and melting skin overwhelmed the earlier sweet aromas of the day.

There was no 9-1-1. No quick response from anyone but us. Mom got Dad to his feet and helped him stumble into the house toward the kitchen, where the phone hung on the wall; and she dialed "0" for the operator, asking to be connected to the police or fire for "Emergency." Kris

82

and I stood and watched with our chins quivering and tears streaming.

Pink and black skin seemed to be melting off Dad's badly charred face and neck as he leaned against the kitchen wall next to the phone, squirming and writhing in pain and moaning uncontrollably. His torn, burned shirt clung to his chest and arms, seared to his body.

While Mom frantically called for the ambulance, I asked, "Dad? Are you all right?"

His slurred response shocked me, "No!—I'm—I'm not—all right!"

At that time in my life, my dad was invincible. Nothing could hurt him. I had never seen him cry. Being the toughest guy I knew, he was my hero in everything, and I looked up to him and admired him. I wanted to be like him. When he told me he was not all right, all I could think of was, "He's going to die." The sight of him transfixed me, and the words he spat out left me cold, fearing I'd never see him again.

Having heard the commotion and screams, the neighbor lady, Alfreida, came over to see if she could help in any way. Mom asked her to take Kris and me while she went to the hospital in the ambulance with Dad. Mom's sister Verna (my cousin Sandy's mom) came to take John.

Dad stayed in the hospital for several weeks, but I don't remember visiting him there. I think Mom and Dad were trying to protect us from the trauma of seeing him, telling us there was a rule against kids being in the hospital as visitors.

The day finally came when Dad was to come home. Mom dropped us off at a friend's and told us she would be by to pick us up after she got Dad. Kris and I were playing with our friends in the front yard of their house, which stood high above the street on a hill, when our red Valiant pulled alongside the curb and honked. Excitedly, I ran halfway down the hill but stopped in my tracks when the image in the front passenger seat became clearer. It was Dad, wrapped in white bandages from the top of his head and down his neck as far as I could see. He tried to turn his head to see me, raised his hand, and weakly waved.

Kris caught up to me and joined me at mid-hill. Standing by the side of the car with the driver's door opened, Mom hollered, "Do you want to come home now or would you like to stay and play for a while?"

Looking at Kris, then at Dad, then back at Kris, I shook my head and quietly said, "No." Then louder, "NO, WE WANT TO STAY FOR AWHILE."

Dad slowly waved again and looked straight out the front windshield of the car. Mom said, "Are you sure? Don't you want to see Dad?"

Kris responded, "We will in a little while. OK?"

"OK. Be home soon," said Mom as she got back into the car and drove off.

I was scared to see him. He looked creepy with those bandages wound around him, and it wasn't what I expected. He looked like the *invisible man* from the movies, all wrapped up like that, and I wondered what would happen when those bandages came off. Would he really be in there? Would it be him? Would I recognize him? I thought he would come home all fixed up, but now I wanted to delay the inevitable for as long as I could. Taking deliberate, almost shuffling steps, the mile-and-a-half walk home took far longer than normal for Kris and me.

For years I had wondered how Dad felt about that. Here he was, coming home from a long stint in the hospital, away from his family and his life. I could only imagine his disappointment when we didn't rush to his side to see him and go home with him. When I asked him about it later in life, he simply said, "I wanted to see you, but I understood."

It still makes me feel sad, especially as a father now. But I acted like the little kid I was at the time. It has stayed with me as a moment to learn from and to be grateful for Dad's presence in my life and his understanding.

*   *   *

Reflection

Strive to value each moment. Actions are taken, things happen, and words are said. All are part of daily life, and all have consequences, good and bad. In an instant, life can be forever changed. It's not unusual for me to go through day after day, managing the rhythm of my life and not seeing all the small pieces that make that rhythm happen; but events such as this remind me not to become too complacent or take any of it for granted.

*   *   *

"Being too good is apt to be uninteresting."
~Harry S. Truman

Chapter Seven

—ᴍ—

Being too good is apt to be uninteresting.

—Harry S. Truman

*Y*outh is full of opportunity for fun and mischief. We learn through trying all kinds of different things, learning lessons and gaining experience in both profound and simple ways. I tried lots of different stuff when I was a kid. I played Little League Baseball, Pony League Football, and Park Board Association Hockey. Dad started me playing golf when I was seven and took me hunting and fishing with my uncles and boy cousins. We never missed a fishing or duck opener. I even became a Cub Scout for a while. I went into it with thoughts of going on swell camping trips, learning to tie all kinds of cool knots that only members of such an elite brotherhood would be able to unknot, and one day standing next to the American flag in my heavily decorated Boy Scout uniform, receiving the highest honor of all, that of an Eagle Scout.

One of our neighborhood moms, Mrs. Swanson, was becoming the den mother for Pack #583, and several of my neighborhood buddies were joining, including Tim, Charlie, and Tony, so I figured I would too. My parents were less keen on it, mainly because of the time commitment. Dad reminded me of my three-month stint as a paperboy, delivering the evening edition of the *Minneapolis Star* to about 40 homes during the week and 107 homes on Sunday mornings at 5:00 a.m., and how I had convinced him that he wouldn't have to be involved at all. As it turned out, I had a hard time getting up that early, especially in winter, and there were many times Mom elbowed Dad out of bed at 4:30 on Sunday mornings to warm up the car and drive me to all my stops so I wouldn't get frostbite. We both got tired of the routine rather quickly, and Dad told me that if I was going to keep the paper route, I was going to have to do it ALL on my own, with no help from him OR my mother. As soon as I found another sap to take it over, I turned in my canvas saddlebag and said good riddance to those early mornings and the three mean dogs down the dead-end lane at the furthest part of my route. They chased me every day.

I assured him this Cub Scout thing was going to be different, that he wouldn't have to be involved at all, except for helping me learn to tie all those swell knots . . . and building a fast, yellow car for the pinewood derby . . . and going on some camping trips with me . . . and attending a few jamborees . . . and teaching me some wrestling moves . . . and . . .

There *were* some things I did on my own to earn those coveted merit badges toward becoming an Eagle Scout. I learned how to cook a wiener on a stick with a sharp point that I carved with a real knife, tie my Cub Scout scarf around my neck, and help old ladies cross the street. I learned that a Cub Scout uniform must always be clean and tucked in and that it is to be worn to school on days when a den meeting, pack meeting, or jamboree was scheduled. Only once did I wear that little navy blue shirt to school, with its few patches, the yellow den numbers, and the little yellow kerchief around its collar. I got ribbed by my friends so much that I vowed to never again wear it in public, so, instead, I would scamper right home after school to quickly change into it on days I had to report to Mrs. Swanson's den.

I was into my third month as a Cub Scout, well on my way to becoming an Eagle Scout, having already earned five merit badges for feats I had accomplished and fears I had overcome, like breathing life-saving oxygen into a plastic dummy named Resuscitation Annie. She wasn't very attractive. I was rather young, and she was rather cold, not really fulfilling any thoughts I may have had of a first kiss, but I planted my schoolboy lips on her anyway and earned a merit badge for it.

There was this little handbook of activities and skills one had to complete in order to earn badges, and all had been fairly easy and routine, until the day of Resuscitation Annie. As creepy as that was, immediately after "kissing" Annie, I was told by Mrs. Swanson it was time to "wrestle Ricky." I shuddered and wondered, with my eyes open wide and a tightening in my throat, what exactly that meant.

After a couple of weird images stopped caroming about in my mind, I realized she was talking about her son Ricky and the two of us engaging in the next merit badge challenge listed in the handbook. She ushered us outside with some diagrams of various moves and wrestling holds and told us she would be watching through the window as we practiced our figure-four leg locks and half nelsons. I thought the wrestling match was to be a demonstration of strategy, moves, and holds, but Ricky had other thoughts. He apparently had read the handbook and with great fervor proceeded to twist me into contortions unknown and indescribable to anyone who has not attempted to earn that particular merit. My three-month mission into becoming an Eagle Scout ended mercilessly in Ricky Swanson's backyard, with his forearm wrapped around my throat and his thighs squeezing my organs into another part of my body, and his mother smiling approvingly through the kitchen window.

While I did earn that last merit badge, I knew being an Eagle Scout was no longer within reach and decided to devote my newfound freedom and extra time to finding ways to show gratitude to my parents for putting up with me.

I used to watch cartoons such as ***Bugs Bunny, Tom and Jerry,*** and ***The Roadrunner.*** The characters were always getting after one another. Someone would step on a rake, have an anvil dropped on his head, slip on a banana peel, get his paws smashed by a hammer, or some other painful yet seemingly harmless misfortune. One of the more regular gags had the antagonist unwittingly sit on a tack and then skyrocket to the ceiling ("YEEEOOWWW!") in pain. There was never any blood. By the time he landed back on the ground, legs were in full cycle, revving up until they hit traction, as he'd take off chasing the perpetrator, who was never caught.

Since dropping an anvil on someone's head was out of the question (where would I get one anyway?), I thought it would be fun to try the tack gag in real life. In deciding who would make the perfect victim, I chose Dad because he not only held a special place in my heart, but he also had the most predictable traffic patterns and habits, which would allow me to devise a plan.

Each day during the week Dad would come home from work at the shop, say a brief hello, and go into the bathroom to clean up. When finished he would make his way into the kitchen to see what Mom was cooking, grab a beverage and the newspaper, and retire to his comfy chair to put his feet up and relax a bit before dinner. Almost every day it was exactly the same—very predictable, very dependable, and very perfect for me and my plan.

With Dad away at work, Mom occupied doing mom-things, and with no one else around, I began my mission and went into the junk drawer for a tack. Once found, I made my way with it to Dad's chair, a recently reupholstered crimson-red wingback chair handed down from one of the grandparents. Mom spent some time carefully selecting the richly colored fabric to create a regal look, with gold paisley patterns swirling through it and gold stitching. With its new look the chair and its matching footstool beamed a vibrant elegance for the 1960s, befitting of a king. I got down on my knees to get a better view of the chair cushion, determining where the best place would be to set the tack. I wanted to be sure it would catch him in the keester region and not in a thigh or somewhere else, so I got down to eye level with the top of the cushion to see if there were indentations from a regular sitting position. There were. I tried to set the pain-inducing tack, but couldn't figure out a way to get it into place so it would stand up and stay that way. I couldn't work the head of the tack under the fabric. I needed a new plan.

Going into Mom's sewing kit, I found, among lots of thread bits and spools of varying colors, a pin cushion that looked like a little red, round cactus with needles and pins sticking out all over it. In examining the various shiny, pointy objects with the interest and skill of a surgeon about to perform a delicate operation, I figured a needle wouldn't work because it couldn't stay standing up properly, but a straight pin with a head could do the trick. I took my little discovery directly to the chair and began working the pin's head through the fabric and into the foam cushion just enough so it would stand straight and remain firmly in place. As I ran my hand across the cushion, I could feel its rigidity and sharp point poking through the thick fabric, about half an inch above the surface. Perfect, I thought. It was barely noticeable when I stepped away.

Our house had a half-wall separating the stairway to the basement from the living room and kitchen. At the top of the stairs a solid little wooden gate could be closed and latched to prevent anyone from accidentally tumbling down, but it also served as a great place to hide if you wanted to pop out and startle someone, or lay in wait for your Dad to come home and sit in his favorite chair to relax (or sit on a pin) after a hard day's work.

This day moved along just like any other. Dad came home at the regular time, said hello, and made his way into the bathroom, while I sat quietly motionless crouched behind the gate of the stairway. When he was finished cleaning up, he walked through the living room and into the kitchen to kiss Mom, find out what was for dinner and grab a beverage before going back to his chair to read the newspaper, exactly as he was supposed to. I listened intently to every step, every word, and every move from behind the gate, sitting low and pressed against it to make myself as small as possible. When I was satisfied he was moving from the kitchen to the living room, I opened the gate ever so quietly and slowly and peeked around the corner as he approached the chair. Mom's back was to me as she hummed an unrecognizable tune and fiddled with dinner at the stove. Dad set his glass down on the lamp table, picked up the paper and shook it open. He turned to sit, his eyes fixed on the front page. My eyes opened wide and bright with anticipation, and I could feel my heart trying to jump out of my chest.

He sat down.

Nothing. Nothing happened. I watched for a few moments and sat still behind the gate, puzzled. *"What went wrong?"* I thought. I sat motionless a bit longer and watched Dad flip through the paper. As he reached for his glass on the table there was a sudden *"OUCH!"* as he leapt out of the chair, followed by a *"What the—??!!"* As he rubbed his right butt cheek and looked at the cushion, Mom ran past me hiding behind the gate and into the living room saying, "What's the matter? What happened?" determined to get to the bottom of it.

He began, "I don't know—I—I was just sitting here reading the paper, and something *bit* me in the butt!"

"How could something bite you there while you're sitting down?" she demanded.

I cupped my hand over my mouth, doing everything I could to keep my laughter silent as Dad looked around the chair and then felt the cushion. He ran his hand across the surface of it and came upon the pin.

"It's a *pin!*" he said incredulously. "Look! It's a pin right here in the cushion, sticking straight up!"

"Well, how could a pin get there like that? The upholsterer would never leave that! And I haven't been doing any sewing or anything. How could—wait a minute. *JEFFREY!*" Mom shouted. (*How did she know it was me?!*)

I began laughing harder until I saw that my parents were *not* laughing at all. My laughter stopped, and my eyes shifted from Dad to Mom, back to Dad, and then to the floor, as I confessed to the misdeed. I was told, in no uncertain terms, that it was *not* all right to do something like that; that real life *isn't* like cartoons; people *aren't* cartoon characters; AND it *wasn't* funny, even if I thought it was.

"In fact," Mom said, after thinking of all the possibilities, "your father could've really been hurt! Why, that pin could have gone right into him, and it might have broken off, and he may have needed surgery to get it out. AND STITCHES! Not to mention lockjaw or rabies! AND TETANUS SHOTS!"

I do believe I wound up with a sorer bottom than he and can say that I have never since put a pin or tack or needle or anything else sharp on someone's seat before he or she sat down. I pulled a few chairs out as someone was about to sit, and I moved a drinking glass or two just as milk was being poured out during dinner, but I definitely learned my lesson on the dangers of sitting on a sharp object. Until now I believe the episode had been largely forgotten.

Many of the fun family times, such as Christmas mornings, were recorded on Super 8 film by Mom and Dad. We four kids would huddle behind the little doors that separated the bedrooms from the living room and wait for the cue from Mom that Dad had the camera and high intensity, retina-burning lights ready to go. We'd stumble into the living room shielding our eyes from impending blindness and squeal with glee to discover what Santa had brought. Those films would be a way for us to later relive the moments and laugh at ourselves and marvel at how young and silly we were.

Other times, like the pin-on-the-chair gag, were not well suited for documenting unless filming could be done clandestinely by a hidden camera, which would have to have been controlled remotely or activated by movement or sense heat or something to start recording the action. One of the years my parents were going out to celebrate their wedding anniversary would have been a great time to have one of those remote controlled cameras hidden discreetly in the dashboard of the car.

They were all dolled up in their finest, she in her polyester floral print dress, pink, high-heeled shoes, and bouffant hairdo; he in his cinnamon brown leisure suit with gold stitching, a paisley print shirt, and white patent leather loafers with the little gold chain across the top. They made their way down our front walk toward the big white 1969 Chrysler 300 with the black vinyl roof, smiled, and waved as they climbed in and drove off to meet their friends at their favorite restaurant, Al & Alma's, which happened to have been founded and run by my mom's Aunt Alma and Uncle

Al. Al was her mother's brother. While changing ownership
over the years, the restaurant still stands and bears the Al &
Alma's name. It has become a local legend as much for its
food as for the difficulty in finding it by car, tucked away
in a modest lakeshore neighborhood of winding, curving
streets that branch off in multiple directions at almost every
bend, surrounded by Lake Minnetonka. Connected to the
"mainland" by a few bridges, the area is aptly called "The
Island" by locals. Finding it by boat is less daunting and is
the preferred mode of transport in summer, but either way
the destination is worth the trip.

As they wound their way around Lake Minnetonka, I
imagine they were enjoying the picturesque drive, sharing
witty conversation, and eagerly anticipating an evening of
laughter and good food with their friends. Both of my parents smoked cigarettes back then, Kent being their brand of
choice, and it was quite common for both of them to light
one up during a car ride. It's a beautiful thought still today,
their sharing of special moments like that.

Savoring their cigarettes somewhere closer to the
restaurant than home, there was a sudden explosion. Dad
jerked the wheel and pulled the car to the side of the road

as Mom frantically brushed away sparks and patted out tiny flames flaring up on and around her.

"What the hell was that?" Dad shouted.

"I don't know! I was just sitting here, and all of the sudden my cigarette blew up and started on fire! Look at my dress!"

(I have this picture in my mind with her hair blown back and her face blackened from gunpowder, the frayed end of the cigarette dangling from her lips and her eyes wide with shock, just like Wile E. Coyote after the dynamite he ordered from ACME explodes on him instead of the Roadrunner.)

The next morning as I got up, I was greeted by a very unhappy mother, toilet paper still wrapped around her bouffant to keep it in shape for church, holding her dress on a hanger in front of me, with burn holes—some large, some small—and the words, "I hope you're happy. You scared me half to death and your father just about drove off the road and into the lake! Look at this dress! I had to go to dinner like this! On our anniversary! Not funny, young man!"

(How did they know it was me?)

Several days, maybe even weeks earlier, I had gone down to the Ben Franklin, the local five and dime store, with my friends and found these little explosive devices that looked like tiny toothpicks designed to be slid into and hidden in the tobacco of a cigarette, pipe, or cigar. I randomly scattered them into a few cigarettes in the packs my parents had about the house, mixing them among the "harmless" regular cigs. I had forgotten all about them until that morning.

What I found amusing wasn't so funny to my parents, and what made it worse for them was the necessary destruction of several other perfectly good cigarettes to find the other devices. I did my duty to help locate the other explosives, but one was still unaccounted for—as best I could remember anyway. So, for several days they smoked with great care and concern that the next cigarette they lit up would be the one that got away, quickly puffing then moving the cigarette far from their faces and clothing, never allowing it to rest in the mouth for too long. Every once in a while one of them would forget and suddenly realize one had been left lazily smoldering in his or her lips and quickly pull it out to arm's length. That strategy mostly worked, and only two more exploded, neither with the surprise or impact of that fateful anniversary night.

*   *   *

Reflection

Be passionate. Be hot or be cold, but not wishy-washy, lukewarm, milquetoast. In whatever I had signed up for, joined, or began, Dad was always pressing me to make certain I was fully committed, that I wasn't going to quit when something became difficult and that I would be in it with passion.

*   *   *

"If you don't know where you're going,
any road will take you there."

~George Harrison

Chapter Eight

Chapter Eight

—∾—

**If you don't know where you're going,
any road will take you there.**

—George Harrison

*F*or as long as I could remember, both of my parents smoked. I thought about that as I considered
Mom's condition and realized she and Dad had smoked
cigarettes probably every day since they were sixteen or
seventeen years old. For over forty years they inhaled that
poison into their lungs, permeating their entire bodies,
mixing with oxygen and getting carried through their
bloodstream, seeping into every nook and cranny from the
tips of their fingers and toes to the muscles and ventricles
of their hearts.

We kids had urged, begged, and nagged them to quit for years. We knew it was bad for them because the surgeon general said so and it was printed on every pack of cigarettes beginning in 1965, but it was more the constant smell we endured than the stated health hazards that drove our relentless assault. At any given hour, from the first thing in the morning until the last light went off at night, there was likely to be a cigarette burning in an ashtray or in someone's mouth. It was bad enough to have that smell in the house but even worse when it was time to take a ride in the family car. There was no escaping it then, especially in winter.

At some point Mom had enough of the nagging and set out to quit. I had given up my bedroom upstairs for John and Paul to share. Mom wanted the TV out of the living room, and with the two young ones in the house we needed another bedroom; so Dad decided to finish the basement. He built walls, creating a family room, a bedroom, a laundry room, a storage closet under the stairs, and a utility room, which housed the furnace and water heater. The concrete floor was covered with linoleum, and the walls were paneled in dark four-by-eight-foot sheets of

veneered maple, after the suspended ceiling with the cor-
rugated fiber panels was installed.

Initially Kris moved her bedroom to the basement, but
she quickly grew tired of having only three walls and no
real privacy. For some reason Dad never built a wall with
a door for the bedroom down there. It was just an open
nook space with the storage closet's louvered bi-fold doors
being one wall as you walked in on the right, the foundation of the house was the back wall, and the new laundry
room formed the wall on the left. When I eagerly agreed
to move down there, I asked Mom if we could find some
way to close off the open wall. We went to a local store
called "The Third Stone," a head shop with record albums,
hookahs, incense, and colored wall hangings of animals
and various scenes of exotic places like India, Mexico,
and New York City, which were displayed alongside lots
of other hippie paraphernalia, much of it unidentifiable by
kids like me and adults like Mom. I don't think Mom was
too comfortable there, but hanging on the wall right next
to the poster of the four Beatles walking in the crosswalk
of Abbey Road were these rolled up bamboo shades. Two
of them would cover the open space perfectly, and they
were long enough to go from ceiling to floor. My friend

Charlie's brother had some just like them in his basement bedroom, and they were really cool, smelling like incense, even though I still wouldn't have a real door.

While those shades provided separation from the TV room, they weren't a good sound barrier, nor were they particularly effective in blocking out all the light. Through the spaces between the bamboo slats I could see the glow and flicker from the television, as Mom and Dad would watch the ten o'clock news and Johnny Carson's monologue. I could hear the voices of newscasts and the laughter from Carson's audience, and occasionally I could hear the muffled conversations my parents would have, though rarely could I make out what they were saying. There were many nights I couldn't fall asleep until they had turned the TV off and gone upstairs to bed.

In particular, my senses were heightened when Mom said she quit smoking. I know she tried, but there were signs all over the place indicating she couldn't quite stay away from the cigarettes. For weeks I had wrestled with how I might confront her or what I would say if I saw her smoking. Dad still smoked and never had any intention of quitting, but Mom tried several times, and it was this time that Kris and I thought her quitting might stick.

As I lay in bed one night, I heard the familiar sound of Dad's lighter firing up and turned to catch a glimpse of my parents through the bamboo blinds. First one red glow appeared and then another. Two cigarette tips burned as smoke began wafting into my little space. I turned away and pulled the covers over my head, not wanting to smell the smoke or face my smoking mother.

Finally, I sat up in bed and said loudly, "I thought you quit!" Almost immediately one of the red glows disappeared as Mom squashed her cigarette out in the ashtray. There was silence for a few moments until Mom came in, sat on the edge of my bed, and said, "I'm sorry. I'm trying to quit, but it is really hard. I'm sorry to have disappointed you." Dad turned the television off, and they went upstairs.

From then on Mom never smoked in front of me, but she continued to smoke right up to the time of her heart attack, never fully able to shake the habit. I didn't know how often or how much she smoked after that incident, but I had to believe it played a part in her heart condition.

* * *

Reflection

Practice forgiveness. I need to forgive myself, just as I should forgive others. Whether unwitting or intentional, I don't always act as I should, nor do I always say the right things. Nobody does. When I was young I did a lot of things I came to regret, but as I got older I began to realize they were all part of growing up. In understanding and practicing the gift of forgiveness and the art of letting go, the load of life becomes lighter.

*   *   *

Decision Time

The doctor returned with a manila envelope and several charts stuffed under his arm. Marianne and a younger man in a similar white coat trailed him. She closed the door and leaned against it with her arms folded across her chest, as the younger man took his place next to Dr. Naswarii. They stood at the head of Mom's bed, and Dr. Naswarii began to speak. As he carefully pulled x-rays from the envelope, he looked squarely at the five of us standing together.

Through all his descriptive meanderings, the core of the message was clear: Mom had massive heart damage that had so weakened her she could not withstand even another slight heart attack, which seemed likely. They could not recommend taking any action in that event. Further, even if she were to survive, she would not be the same person because of the estimated length of time her brain had been without oxygen. She would not be able to talk, or walk, or take care of herself. None of us would be living a "normal" life again. We were to discuss signing a "Do Not Resuscitate" order.

Death. This was so sudden, so final. At one moment I was thinking of my life with her, and the next I was thinking of life without her. In another moment still, I was thinking of her without life, being held together with machines and medicines. I thought about Dad. What would this mean for him? What about my kids and the other grandchildren?

Disbelief was beginning to be replaced by anger. There was talk of being cheated. Everyone was being cheated. It wasn't her time to go! She was still young at sixty-two years old! I always considered myself fortunate, having grown up knowing my grandparents, and I desperately wanted the same for my kids. It was one of the main reasons we were moving back home: to be closer to them.

This stark, cold hospital room had been sent into a chaotic tangle of negative thoughts. Half-sentences and questions were thrown about as randomly as they came to our minds. It seemed we were being told to "pull the plug," that her life no longer held value or hope. It seemed they were telling us they had done all they could. Were they telling us that? Had they really done all they could?

The doctor finally spoke up, saying, "No one is giving up hope, but there is not much more we can do if she goes into cardiac arrest again." He was fearful her heart could not take the stress of putting the paddles to her yet again. We were to decide, as a family, what course of action the hospital was to take under that circumstance. He explained the risks of both action and inaction, but he could not be certain of results in either case. "One thing I do know," Dr. Naswarii stated, "is that your mom is very weak and her system simply will not withstand any more strain or stress."

Do Not Resuscitate. Those words rang loudly in my head, over and over again.

*   *   *

*"Experience is simply the name
we give our mistakes."*
~Oscar Wilde

Chapter Nine

Chapter Nine

—◦◦◦—

Experience is simply the name we give our mistakes.

—Oscar Wilde

When Mom and I were rummaging through the keepsake box and memory books prior to their move, she came across a yellowed newspaper clipping tucked between some pages of my baby book. There was no journal entry, no writings or notes, just the folded article. I watched with interest and asked her what it was as she carefully unfolded it and straightened each crease. She said nothing as she held the article for both of us to read. The headline was "Narrow Escape for 10 Year Old Boy."

It was a brief article, maybe four paragraphs long. We both read through it in silence.

I rode my bike over to my friend Tim's house, which was less than a mile away. I had gone there dozens of times, riding up the slight incline of our road to the intersection where the county road crossed, always checking both directions for traffic, and pedaling across to the other side, where large pine and spruce trees lined one side of the quiet lane down to Tim's house.

On that particular day I was to be home by 4:30 p.m. so I could get something to eat and have time to get ready for my Little League game at 6:00. As happens with kids, the afternoon flew by, and suddenly I was late. I hopped on my little stingray bike with the fake leopard skin, banana-shaped seat, grabbed the butterfly handlebars, and pedaled up Tim's hill as fast as I could. At the top I pedaled faster to gain more speed down the gradual decline to the county road and, ultimately, my house.

At that hour every weekday the local factory, Tonka Toys, ended a shift, and the county road served as one of the main arteries to move workers home. The flow of traffic was regular and predictable, as sedan and pickup truck tires hummed their way along the two-lane asphalt road on their way west toward rural country. That sound was unmistakable and so routine that you'd always know when it was between 4:30 and 4:45 in the afternoon, whether you had a watch or not.

Many times riding toward that county road from Tim's house I had tried to peek through the branches and needles of the big evergreens to catch a glimpse of the oncoming traffic. Not only could I hear humming tires, but I could usually see a flash of chrome or glint of color as the cars approached. Vehicles coming from the other direction were easy to see because only a modest, single-story house stood on that corner of the intersection. The evergreen branches hung low and full on the right, so I always slowed down to a roll or came to a complete stop to make sure it was safe to cross.

This time was different. I was late. I didn't know exactly what time it was, but I knew I was late. I continued to pedal and speed toward the intersection. When I approached the evergreens, I stopped pedaling so I could listen for tires. I heard nothing at first. Then I heard the familiar hum, caught a flash of chrome through the trees, and watched as a blue sedan zoomed by. Quiet again. The car disappeared toward the west. I continued to coast, ear tuned to the road. I heard nothing. I saw nothing coming from the west and nothing through the branches from the east.

Satisfied it was clear, I pedaled again, hoping to gain enough speed to catch some air off the rise where the lane met the road. I continued to listen and look but pedaled even faster as I focused on the challenge. I passed the evergreens and immediately realized I was not alone in the road.

I slammed my right foot backward on the pedal and felt the bike begin to slide out from under me as the grill of the oncoming car barreled toward me. Tires wailed an ear-splitting screech, and in that very instant I saw the terrified faces of the women in the car, their eyes and mouths open wide. Trying frantically to stop, I slid sideways onto the asphalt, let go of the handlebars and tumbled.

There were screams. The left side of my body burned in pain; and as I opened my eyes, I found I had landed directly beneath the front of the car, between the two front tires. Panicked, nervous feet bounced out of all four doors as frightened female voices filled the air all around me. I began to crawl out, wriggling through the blood pooled beneath me. One woman, the driver, begged me through her tears to stay still and ordered someone else to call for help.

I knew the car didn't hit me. She wasn't so sure. In a matter of moments a small crowd of neighborhood kids and parents had gathered, and a police car appeared on the scene. Traffic was being routed slowly around the stalled sedan with the bicycle wedged beneath its right front tire. In another moment the rescue squad pulled up. By this time the policeman was trying to get a clear picture of the situation by asking the matronly women, each wrapped in muted floral print dresses and wearing white sneakers, what had happened. They stated hysterically, emphatically, but simply, "He appeared from nowhere! There was no time to react! It's a wonder he wasn't killed!"

I couldn't argue the facts. After being cleaned up and bandaged by the paramedics, I was escorted by the policeman and mildly reprimanded in front of the ladies, who were still visibly shaken. They all were relieved at the outcome, and I apologized through my tears, both of pain and fear. The officer took down all the information from those involved and then took me home and waited with me on the front steps until Mom and Dad returned from wherever they were. He gave them the facts, knowing full well my parents understood precisely what to do next. I can't seem to remember exactly what my punishment was, but I missed my baseball game.

After reading the article, Mom said, "You were lucky."

I said plainly, "I was stupid."

Tears welled up in Mom's eyes, and after a pause she said, "You scared us."

"I know I did. I'm sorry. Still."

*　*　*

Reflection

Slow down, and look both ways. Life happens fast, and while I can never be sure things will happen or work out as I have hoped, planned, or been told, much is still in my hands if I take the time to see it and grab hold of it.

*　*　*

With that recently shared moment fresh in my mind, I thought about how my parents must have felt. I thought about my own children and shuddered at the thought of losing one of them. A feeling of guilt made me hang my head as I relived the experience again, this time as a parent.

I felt selfish. I felt selfish and guilty about so much. I was thinking about myself and what I was losing. I had been angry about what we would all be losing.

As I held my head in my hands, I looked up to see Dad standing, gently stroking Mom's hair, and looking sorrowfully resigned. I lowered my head again and began to pray, wondering what to do, feeling helpless, alone, abandoned by God. I had felt helpless before.

*   *   *

"Only the sculptor's hand can break the spell to free the figures slumbering in the stone."
~Michelangelo

Chapter Ten

Chapter Ten

—⟋⟍—

Only the sculptor's hand can break the spell to free the figures slumbering in the stone.

—Michelangelo

When I was seventeen years old, a junior in high school, as full as my life was, it seemed entirely empty. It was strange. I was a good student, although I certainly could have applied myself more. I had lots of friends, went on dates, played sports, and was even president of the junior class. I was busy, as I had always been, but somehow I was not happy. I didn't know why. What I did know was that nothing was fun. Nothing was interesting, even as my friends continued to include me in their plans.

One Friday night I was all set to go out with a group of my buddies. I didn't feel like going, but they pleaded and cajoled and told me it would be fun, so I agreed to go.

Unmotivated and trying to think of a way out, I lollygagged in getting ready. I certainly didn't think I was going to be much fun and what was planned (going to some dance club for teens) sounded pretty lame. The rest of the family was already out somewhere, with Mom and Dad having left instructions for me on when to be home.

I was alone in the house, wandering about aimlessly from room to room and chair to chair, waiting for Bruce and Bobby to pick me up. Soon I saw the headlights in the driveway and looked out the window to see the two of them bounding up the steps and walkway toward the door. Before they could knock, I opened the door and said, "I'm not going." This wasn't the first time. I had been in a funk for a while, and they were growing tired of it. They tried, once, to convince me to join them. I meekly said, "No. I'm going to stay home."

Bruce's next words stung me and have stuck with me. "You used to be fun, man. What has happened to you? You know what? You've become a real drag. See ya later." With that I closed the front door, and they walked down the

130

steps shaking their heads. I watched through the curtains as they pulled out of the driveway and left. Our friendship was never the same again.

I went back to my bedroom, turned off the lights and lay face down on my bed. I still don't know why I was so sad and disinterested. After a while I got up and fumbled through my jeans pockets to find the five dollars I had borrowed from Dad earlier in the week. I walked into the kitchen and sat at the table with a small notepad, a pen, and the money. Through my tears I wrote a note to my parents, returning the five dollars and apologizing for my attitude. In a sense I felt I was writing a note of finality—a note releasing a well of emotion pushed down inside me for many weeks. I was crying, but for what? I still could not put those feelings and emotions into words. I finished the little note by just apologizing again and confessing I did not know what was happening to me.

My head was aching, wishing I wasn't alone but at the same time not wanting to be with anyone. I put an album on my stereo's turntable, Crosby, Stills, Nash & Young's "Déjà Vu," and lying face down in my bed I listened to their harmonies, distinctively theirs, as they sang, "Carry on. Love is coming. Love is coming to us all."

I didn't feel worthless, but felt I wasn't worthy of anyone's friendship, support, or love. If people knew what was in my head, the things I thought about and even some of the things I did, they would know I was a fraud. They would know I wasn't really the person I seemed to be on the outside. No one really knew me but me. And my friends were all too good for me. That's what I thought. I couldn't understand why they wanted to be my friends, and I even kind of resented them for not knowing better. I couldn't understand why my family still seemed to love me, why they continued to embrace me even as I tried to push them farther and farther away.

Time passed, and I was in and out of sleep when my door opened. It was Dad. Cautiously he entered my room, his image silhouetted by the light coming from the hallway. He sat on the end of my bed and asked, "Jeff? What is wrong? What's going on?" I sat up, saying, "I don't know," and looked away, down at the floor. He put his hand on my shoulder, and I reached for him and hugged him, crying again and saying, "I don't know. I don't know."

The more I tried to explain and make sense of what I was feeling and what I was going through, the more confusing it sounded. Dad shook his head, frustrated he didn't

132

have an answer for me. I didn't really expect one. He left the room hugging me and saying, "Let's figure it out."

In the morning I got up late and groggily padded into the kitchen. Mom was there, alone at the table with a cup of coffee. I sat down with some orange juice, and after a few minutes of awkward silence, she asked me, "What's wrong?" Through it all, the message was the same: I did not know. She asked me if I had been praying, talking to God.

"Oh boy," I thought, *"Here comes another one of her Bible discussions—just what I need."*

"I did for awhile," I said, half making it up, "but nothing changed. God's not listening to me."

Mom corrected me, saying, "Oh. Well, that happens to be one of the things God does really well. He always listens. He'll never leave your side, whether you know it or not. He is always there for you, and He knows you better than you know yourself. If you don't think you can talk to Him in prayer, try writing to Him. Find Him."

"Yeah. Right," I said and got up and left.

"And Jeffrey," she said before I got away, "we love you. No matter what you are going through, no matter what you do, and no matter what you may think, we love you because of who you are. No matter what. And so does God. And that love will never change or ever go away."

That was the shortest "Bible discussion" she ever laid on me. I had often been intimidated by her seemingly unshakable faith in God. There were times I resented her for it. I resented her pushing it on me and making me feel guilty for not thinking, feeling, and believing the same way.

Mid-afternoon Monday I was sitting in one of the cubicles in the English Resource Center at school. We had open periods each day, and students were supposed to use the time wisely for study or projects in the proper resource area for the specific subject one was working on. Off in thought, I was staring lazily into the wood grain of the desk, where Brett had scrawled his everlasting love for Susie (they were already dating others by that time) and someone known only as "Mad Dog" had carved his disdain for one of the teachers right alongside a blue-inked cross. The cross caught my attention, and I remembered what Mom had said. I hesitated but then opened my yellow-covered spiral notebook to a blank page and began writing, "Dear God . . ." For the next several days, into weeks, I wrote every chance I could and soon had many pages of letters and notes to God on everything that was going on in my life, as well as everything I hoped for. I could write a conversation with no fear of judgment or lecture. I was free to be me, exactly who I was and where I was at that time in my life.

Some of the entries trailed off, and some of the letters and words ran together, and some of the writing was just plain illegible, but the thoughts were there. I still have them, tucked away in a box with other memorabilia from my youth.

Eventually, my writing to God helped pull me out of my funk, and I began to reengage my life, moving on as though nothing had happened. Nothing more was said. No great revelations occurred. I went about with my friends and on with my high school youth with enthusiasm—as it should be—and to this point I remember mainly the good things, which far outnumbered the bad and the indefinable.

Much later in my life I learned from Mom and Dad just how frightened they were, how out of control they felt in not being able to understand what was going on with me. I could not fully fathom what I was going through then, but I realize now it was teenage depression sweeping through my thoughts and into my every action of day-to-day life. I was bored with everything, including myself, but mostly I felt entirely lost in who I was and what was expected of me. Little did I understand that the expectations others had of me were quite basic and easy to fulfill by just being a committed student, a dependable friend, and a good son.

The teenage expectations I had placed on myself were somehow beyond what I felt I could deliver. I convinced myself that others thought about me, and expected of me, far more than they did. During those days and weeks, I was unable to be content in living each day with eager anticipation of whatever may come, and I languished instead with a morbid tendency to dwell on matters of all sorts over which I had no control. And I looked for and clung to the worst that all my young life had to offer.

When I finally grew weary of my own misery and sought desperate relief through writing, expressing whatever I was thinking and feeling to God, I found that I could accept myself because He did. And so did my friends and family.

* * *

Reflection

Seek God. Surrendering can be liberating. Realizing I cannot do it all by myself all the time was a big step in finding the path to freeing my mind from guilt, thoughts of inadequacy, and feelings of tedium and loneliness. I have learned that at any time and at all times I can meet God where He is, which is wherever I am.

*   *   *

"When the solution is simple, God is answering."
~Albert Einstein

Chapter Eleven

Chapter Eleven

—◊—

When the solution is simple, God is answering.

—Albert Einstein

s I remembered Mom's words, "Find Him," I began to pray in earnest. The exercise I had gone through years earlier had taught me that seeking God does help, in a very real sense. It worked for me then, and I was again desperate for help, though I felt a little ashamed for being an on-again/off-again pray-er throughout my life.

I got up and moved to Mom's side and held her hand. I prayed while holding onto her. As the others in the room continued with their quiet conversations, I sat for several moments in deep conversational thought with God and

Mom. I prayed for her health, and I prayed for her soul, and I prayed for my Dad and our family. And I prayed for my strength and understanding. I sat still with my head bowed and did not get it. Why? Why was this happening? I was tired and couldn't think much more, other than that I had done nothing.

Nothing. I felt quiet, exhausted, disconnected. And I felt resigned.

As certain as I am of my words in those prayers and my thoughts in those moments, I am equally certain I felt God touch me as I paused to rest, with my head hanging low against the back of Mom's hand. Warmth, a palpable, undeniable feeling of warmth, stirred me, beginning with a sense that someone else's hand was suddenly resting on top of mine. Tension left my hands and wrists; and as I felt the softness of my mother's palm, a welling of emotion lifted from deep within me. There was a distinct warming of my entire body, and my heavy heart began to lighten. I was filled with an unmistakable sense of peace. I suddenly felt comfort—and certain knowledge. My anger and my fear had been replaced by a calm knowing, an understanding.

What had been so complicated suddenly became quite simple: It was not for me to ask why but only to trust, to let go, to trust God with my mother.

Comfort came in realizing that her life was not at all mine to claim. This was no longer to be about me or anyone else. It was her life, and her life was God's. She was God's child. She always had been and I, we—all who knew her—had been blessed by the gift of life God had given her. I was assured that the angels were with her, holding her as she slept, ready to help her find the path. With my eyes closed, still cradling her hand as she lay unconscious, I quite vividly saw her in God's warmth and light and love, knowing that if He were to reach out and call her home, she would surely, joyously, embrace Him. After all, that had always been her goal: to be with God. If, however, it was not her time, I knew she would fight with all her strength to come back to us. She would do whatever God asked of her. She was that way. She had complete faith.

* * *

Reflection

Let go. Changing, leaving, moving on, and trusting are not easy. They require a loosening of my grip, my control, and believing that through God I can handle what is to come, regardless of what that may be. New circumstances always provide new opportunities for learning and growing, though often I still find that difficult to see and realize early on.

*   *   *

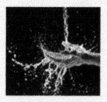

"Life is a succession of lessons which must be lived to be understood."
~Helen Keller

Chapter Twelve

Chapter Twelve

—✺—

**Life is a succession of lessons which
must be lived to be understood.**

—Helen Keller

*A*nd now it was time for me. I had learned from
my mother, and in these days I began to realize
just how much. This event, this experience had neatly led
me to bits and pieces of my life I had not recalled for years
and took me down a path to rediscover what lessons I was
to have learned. The memories were always there, but
some of the meanings behind them had been hidden until
they could be found through my need to understand.

It's like a painting that has hung on the wall for years.
You can walk by it time after time without notice, or look at

it from across the room; and then one day you see a different detail, a different angle of light, a different emphasis of color, and you never again look at the painting the same way.

My old lessons had become clearer, more meaningful, as they were framed by this new experience. I felt blessed. My understanding, my faith and trust, had come from how those lessons were taught. I never saw Mom's faith waver, though I'm sure she had her times. My parents never gave up on me. They were steadfast in raising me, teaching me, and laying the foundation of God within me, regardless of my willingness to accept it.

As my children continue to grow, learn, and experience, I am now more aware of how I help them along. I try to be more careful with my words and more eager with my hugs. Sometimes I find myself wishing I had handled things differently. Often, I wonder which of their lessons they will remember later on in their lives.

And how they will view them.
And how they will view me.

I settled in for the long flight home and rested my eyes. All these things came back to me, and I was compelled to write, just as I had in my teenage journals to God. This journey had taken me much farther than just the miles traveled, yet it was much closer to home than I could have ever imagined, and I ached to be home where I could feel safe and warm, comforted by the familiarity I had experienced in my youth and still longed for.

That familiarity of home and the lessons of long ago had been little more than distant memories stashed away in the recesses of my subconscious. But there they were again, brought to memory, teaching me anew when needed most. I found myself drawn to reflection because the time was right, but my thoughts ran where they wanted to. In the confining terms of coming to grips with my mother's mortality, I had the relative freedom to ponder my expectations, my feelings, and my faith. Emotions ran wild through my mind over several days, unfettered by many other distractions.

This unexpected circumstance was far beyond my control, and making sense out of those kinds of things remains elusive much of the time. My constant challenge now is not only *finding* time to examine, reflect, and pray but actually *using* that time for those purposes. I remind myself to look deeper than the surface, beyond the issue of the moment, and focus on what can be learned. Comfort and understanding can come from the least expected sources and the least desired circumstances, but if my heart and mind are open to receive, they do come.

From God.

As I opened my eyes on the flight home and turned toward the jet window to view the night sky, the stars danced in their brilliant light, and the crescent moon, God's fingernail, again reminded me that in the quietest of moments, in the loneliest of thoughts, and in the grandest of celebrations, God is with me.

Always.

Reward lies in faith.

Miracles do happen.

*   *   *

Reflection

Expect the unexpected. With God all things are possible.

*   *   *

"Anyone who does not believe in miracles is not a realist."
~David Ben-Gurion

Epilogue

Epilogue

—◊—

Anyone who does not believe in miracles is not a realist.

—David Ben-Gurion

*A*fter eleven days of vigil, waiting, saying goodbye, and seeing no apparent improvement, Mom inexplicably and unexpectedly awoke, mumbling something about being thirsty. Dr. Naswarii was tracked down by Nurse Marianne, as we all surrounded her and hugged her and kissed her. Within minutes the doctor came hurriedly in with eyebrows raised and stood at her bedside in amazement. He took her hand and said, "Hello, Patty." She looked at him with eyes half open and whispered weakly and slowly, "Hello. Who are you? Did you bring coffee?"

She then said, "Hey—Stinky!" We all looked at each other, wondering which of us she meant. (I pointed at Paul, but for some reason they all ended up looking at me.)

The doctor smiled, and we cried. "This is a miracle," he said hesitatingly. "You are an amazing woman. We thought we had lost you. You fooled us."

She defied death. She defied the doctors. She had not suffered the predicted setbacks of further heart strain, and the fluid around her heart had lessened. She awoke that morning to the shock of the doctors and the joy of her family. Initially, we were still unsure of her prospects for life, let alone her quality of life. Her improvement came slowly at first, but the doctors shifted their outlook and prognosis after learning she had not suffered brain damage, only the loss of some hearing and the functioning of 70 percent of her heart.

We knew early on that a prayer chain had been started by friends from Mom and Dad's church, and it spread literally around the world into a massive network of people praying on behalf of my mother and family. It is an amazing thing to experience that kind of outpouring of love and support, getting reports, updates, and well wishes through emails and voicemails from people we didn't even know. It was overwhelming and humbling, and I am grateful to all who kept us in their prayers.

I was ready to accept Mom's passing. I went through a process of letting go, saying goodbye, and grieving, but then the unexpected happened—she opened her eyes. It was nothing any of us were prepared for. While I had experienced the miracle of my mother's survival from certain death, through my desperate search for answers, I experienced the personal miracle of God touching me, my heart, my mind, and my soul. I came to better understand the power of life's lessons and the value they hold. I was blessed by my mother's near death, by gaining a deeper sense of life. The lessons I learned early on formed my foundation, and reconsidering them as an adult helped me refocus my goals, my aspirations, and myself.

Prayers are answered in many different ways and not always in the ways I hope or think they should be. I typically ask for the obvious and the easiest, what's right in front of me. But asking God for wisdom and understanding sheds light on otherwise dark corners, situations, and perspectives of life. My personal gift from God, my answered prayer, came in the understanding and peace I received. Mom's survival and recovery was God's gift to all of us. Truly, she is a miracle of God today, just as she was at her birth and throughout her life. Each of us is a miracle of God in ways difficult to fully comprehend. Mom's zest and appreciation for life have never been stronger, and she is living as an example of what it can mean to know God and live life fully.

Over several weeks, into months, she recovered, regaining strength despite the loss of heart muscle. Now, more than a decade later, Mom is active as ever, enjoying her twelve grandchildren, volunteering every moment she can, and playing occasional rounds of golf with Dad.

A couple of years after her recovery, Mom and Dad made a trip back to the hospital's intensive care unit to greet and thank the doctors and nursing staff personally for the care she received during those weeks. Surprised and overjoyed to see her, Marianne and the other nurses hugged Mom, saying, "Miracle Patty is here!" They were so very grateful Mom and Dad would take the time to visit them, telling them they never get to see patients after they leave intensive care.

"You left quite an imprint on the unit and those of us who worked with you," Marianne said, "especially me. I know miracles happen because I know you."

That got me thinking. The impact we have on other lives is mostly unknown. We go through our day-to-day tasks and interactions without giving much thought to how someone else might be affected by who we are, what we do, and what we say. In a strange twist, here were my parents visiting the hospital and intensive care unit to thank them for their care, and they received unexpected gratitude from the nurses, who felt *privileged* to have tended to my mother because of what they experienced and witnessed.

Most of the time we are wrapped up in our own world, doing our own thing. We are focused on chopping through our own life's jungle to forge our own path through each day. Rarely do we take the time or have the sensitivity to actively engage our brains toward thinking about how we might be impacting someone else's day, let alone someone else's life. Yet, I'm quite certain most of us can identify with Nurse Marianne's very clear recognition of the impact Mom had on her life. I can imagine how she must have felt having watched us, and on some level traveled with us, through that journey of emotions over those many days.

157

And I can imagine her own amazement and joy when Mom awoke that morning.

Somehow we can remember circumstances and individuals making a difference in our lives, but we have very little clue about the impact we have had on others. That is, unless we are told.

I again learned something, magnified by the circumstances surrounding me. Taking the time and energy to recognize and thank others for what they have meant to me, in my life, would never again be put off to a more convenient time. It would be handled as a priority as soon as possible after the moment it entered my mind. Many individuals probably have no idea how much the intersection of our lives impacted me, and it doesn't matter if they feel the same way; I'm not out fishing for compliments or wanting to create a mutual admiration society. But for me it needs to be done on purpose, not just as a result of running into someone in the grocery store or post office. No, this is very personal and needs to be written down and sent, as in a letter or note, preferably handwritten and certainly in my own words, although a personalized greeting card or even an email can be a start. A well-thought-out phone call or a face-to-face meeting over lunch or coffee could do as well, but a letter or note seems to lend a bit more permanency to the effort. And it is important to be able to define exactly what that impact was. It wouldn't be sufficient to say, "You know, I'm really glad I had you as a teacher." I must be more specific than that. It must include the "because you. . ." in order to be meaningful to the other person. I need to convey an "I-know-miracles-happen-because-I-know-you" kind of gratitude for being part of my life.

What has impact for someone may be as simple as well-chosen words or an arm around a shoulder at the right moment. Or it might be a conscious decision to recognize an individual in your life's sphere, as my wife Heidi did at a young age.

There were a lot of kids to play with while she was growing up in her neighborhood. As they grew older, two brothers were living through a dysfunctional family with drugs, alcohol, and abuse, and they drifted, withdrawing from normal interactions. One of them went away, while the other continued through school, though seemingly sullen and rather alone, involved in drugs himself. Although Heidi's life was much different, she made the decision to regularly say hello to Matt when she passed him in the hallway at school. If they were walking in the same direction, she would often walk with him as others avoided him. After all, they played together when younger and still lived in the same neighborhood. She couldn't pretend she didn't know him.

Many years later Matt ran into Heidi's parents. They didn't recognize him at first. He was no longer the troubled neighborhood kid they once knew. He was clean and sober, married and raising a family. Matt apologized for his actions and attitude as a rambunctious youth and felt bad for any trouble he and his family caused the neighbors. But then he told them one of the reasons he was able to make it through those days. In the loneliest of times during his tortured youth, Heidi greeted him as a friend. He looked forward to her kind wave, her warm hello, and her soft smile—her recognition of him as a person. Going through drug rehabilitation and counseling, those were some of the thoughts and memories from his youth that held value for him. He was so very grateful for Heidi's presence in his life. She had no idea.

This little book started out as a way for me to recount the days, chronicle my journey through the lessons of my youth, and remember how God touched me in that very significant moment at Mom's bedside. It was a way for me to share this personal experience, revelation, and gift with my family. Over the years the story grew as I continued to explore my emotions, life's memories, and that powerful experience during those days. It is a feeling I will never forget, but even still I have a hard time explaining the breadth and depth, the magnitude of what I felt, for it is far beyond anything I experienced prior or since. It was a profound awakening and a dawning of understanding of a larger piece of life and of God. It was a realigning of my perspective to once again appreciate the lessons I have learned and to set my sight on a wider view: that we all have the ability and the responsibility to affect one another in ways that bring each other closer to God and to help others have the life experience they deserve, even through seemingly simple interactions, by offering the very best we have.

Through the strong foundation of my parents, through the examples they set, and through their unwillingness to stray from core values and beliefs, my childhood understanding of God has come full circle. And I am reminded each time I see God's fingernail.

References

—⁓—

Chapter One: **"Life is what happens to you while you are busy making other plans."** — John Lennon (1940-1980), musician, artist.

From the song "Beautiful Boy" by John Lennon, on the disc album *Double Fantasy* released 1980 by EMI Records.

Chapter Two: **"I remember my mother's prayers and they have clung to me all my life."** — Abraham Lincoln (1809-1865), American president.

Abraham Lincoln. BrainyQuote.com, Xplore Inc, 2010. http://www.brainyquote.com/quotes/quotes/a/abraha-mlin145909.html (accessed July 12, 2010).

Chapter Three: **"A hero is someone who understands the responsibility that comes with freedom."** — Bob Dylan (1941-), musician, poet.

Bob Dylan. BrainyQuote.com, Xplore Inc, 2010. http://www.brainyquote.com/quotes/quotes/b/bobdylan142058.html (accessed July 12, 2010).

Chapter Four: **"I don't like that man. I must get to know him better."** — Abraham Lincoln (1809-1865), American president.

Abraham Lincoln. BrainyQuote.com, Xplore Inc, 2010. http://www.brainyquote.com/quotes/quotes/a/abrahamlin104175.html (accessed July 12, 2010).

Chapter Five: **"Take care of all your memories, for you cannot relive them."** — Bob Dylan (1941 -), musician, poet.

Bob Dylan. BrainyQuote.com, Xplore Inc, 2010. http://www.brainyquote.com/quotes/quotes/b/bobdylan142081.html (accessed July 12, 2010).

Chapter Six: **"Nothing is more memorable than a smell."** —Diane Ackerman (1948-), American poet.

Diane Ackerman. BrainyQuote.com, Xplore Inc, 2010. http://www.brainyquote.com/quotes/quotes/d/dianeacker106723.html (accessed July 12, 2010).

Chapter Seven: **"Being too good is apt to be uninteresting."** — Harry S. Truman (1884-1972), American president.

Harry S. Truman. BrainyQuote.com, Xplore Inc, 2010. http://www.brainyquote.com/quotes/quotes/h/harrystru153780.html (accessed July 12, 2010).

Chapter Eight: **"If you don't know where you're going, any road will take you there."** — George Harrison (1943-2001), musician.

George Harrison. From the song "Any Road" by George Harrison on the disc album *Brainwashed*, released 2002 by Umlaut Corp., licensed to EMI Records.

Chapter Nine: **"Experience is simply the name we give our mistakes."** — Oscar Wilde (1854-1900), Irish dramatist.

Oscar Wilde. BrainyQuote.com, Xplore Inc, 2010. http://www.brainyquote.com/quotes/quotes/o/oscarwilde105029.html (accessed July 12, 2010).

Chapter Ten: **"Only the sculptor's hand can break the spell to free the figures slumbering in the stone."** — Michelangelo (1475-1564), artist, sculptor.

Michelangelo. BrainyQuote.com, Xplore Inc, 2010. http://www.brainyquote.com/quotes/quotes/m/michelange402372.html (accessed July 12, 2010).

Chapter Eleven: **"When the solution is simple, God is answering."** — Albert Einstein (1879-1955), German physicist.

Albert Einstein. BrainyQuote.com, Xplore Inc, 2010. http://www.brainyquote.com/quotes/quotes/a/alberteins148826.html (accessed July 12, 2010).

Chapter Twelve: **"Life is a succession of lessons which must be lived to be understood."** — Helen Keller (1880-1968), American author.

Helen Keller. BrainyQuote.com, Xplore Inc, 2010. http://www.brainyquote.com/quotes/quotes/h/helenkelle103524.html (accessed July 12, 2010).

Epilogue: **"Anyone who does not believe in miracles is not a realist."** — David Ben-Gurion (1896-1973), Israeli statesman, Israel's first prime minister.

David Ben-Gurion. BrainyQuote.com, Xplore Inc, 2010. http://www.brainyquote.com/quotes/quotes/d/david-beng387794.html (accessed July 12, 2010).

Self-Reflection Guide

—ຓ—

*A*s stated in the *Introduction*, the memories, expe-riences, and lessons you have just read form the cornerstones of my foundation. But they are just that: *my* reflections forming *my* foundation. This guide may help you explore and realize some of your own.

1) Life rarely plays out exactly how we have planned, thought, or wished it would. Think of some instances when your life plans had to change.

2) We have all had individuals to whom we have looked up and admired; what people have had a positive influ-ence in your life? Who are they for you?

3) We are all human, with our own flaws and shortcom-ings. The trick is finding the good in others, as well as

within ourselves. Have there been times when finding the good in someone has been a challenge?

4) We all have unique memories forming our unique perspective on things. What are some of yours?

5) No one can live your life for you. Your memories are yours. The lessons you have learned are yours. Who do you need to thank for being a part of your life? Why? Be specific. This is a start to your list of letters to people who have had an impact in your life.

6) As you continue to move through your days and years, what are your greatest hopes and dreams for yourself and for those you love?

7) What are some steps you plan to take for yourself after reading and reflecting on your own life through *God's Fingernail*?

Think of the kinds of things you can do to help those you love and those you meet to have the kind of life experience they *deserve* and not just what they expect. Your life will be forever changed, and so may theirs, because the light of God will shine through you.